Caryl Churchill

'This is the book about Caryl Churchill I have been waiting for! Mary Luckhurst does several things brilliantly. She relates Churchill's plays to their cultural and political context, shows how their formal experimentation is dictated by ideas and analyzes their performance history through the words of the practitioners. I learned an amazing amount.'
Michael Billington, *author and theatre critic for* The Guardian

'Mary Luckhurst has become the doyenne of research by inter-view. She reveals the processes of actors and directors working on Churchill's plays in ways that are brilliantly enlightening.'
Derek Paget, *University of Reading*

Mary Luckhurst is Professor of Artistic Research and Creative Practice at the University of Melbourne. She co-founded the Department of Theatre, Film and Television and is Honorary Professor at the University of York (UK) and is both a National Teaching Fellow and an International Scholar for the Higher Education Academy (UK). She is a theatre historian, writer and director and is a world expert in analysing the processes of acting, directing and performance writing. Her many books include *Dramaturgy: A Revolution in Theatre*; *Theatre and Celebrity in Britain 1660–2000*; *On Acting*; *On Directing*; and *Playing for Real: Actors on Playing Real People*. Her latest book, *Theatre and Ghosts: Materiality, Performance and Modernity* (2014), marries theatre with spectrality studies. She is currently working on *Theatre and Human Rights after 1945: Things Unspeakable*.

Routledge modern and contemporary dramatists
Edited by Maggie B. Gale and Mary Luckhurst

Routledge Modern and Contemporary Dramatists is a new series of innovative and exciting critical introductions to the work of internationally pioneering playwrights. The series includes recent *and* well-established playwrights and offers primary materials on contemporary dramatists who are under-represented in secondary criticism. Each volume provides detailed cultural, historical and political material, examines selected plays in production, and theorises the playwright's artistic agenda and working methods, as well as their contribution to the development of playwriting and theatre.

Volumes currently available in the series are:

J. B. Priestley *by Maggie B. Gale*
Federico Garcia Lorca *by Maria M. Delgado*
Susan Gaspell and Sophie Treadwell *by Jerry Dickey and Barbara Oziebo*
August Strindberg *by Eszter Szalczer*
Anton Chekhov *by Rose Whyman*
Maria Irene Fornes *by Scott T. Cummings*

Future volumes will include:

Mark Ravenhill *by John F. Deeney*
Brian Friel *by Anna McMullan*
Sarah Kane *by Chris Megson*

Caryl Churchill

Routledge modern and
contemporary dramatists

Mary Luckhurst

Routledge
Taylor & Francis Group

LONDON AND NEW YORK

First published 2015
by Routledge
2 Park Square, Milton Park, Abingdon, Oxon OX14 4RN

and by Routledge
711 Third Avenue, New York, NY 10017

Routledge is an imprint of the Taylor & Francis Group, an informa business

British Library Cataloguing in Publication Data
A catalogue record for this book is available from the British Library

Library of Congress Cataloging-in-Publication Data
Luckhurst, Mary.
Caryl Churchill / by Mary Luckhurst.
pages cm. – (Routledge modern and contemporary dramatists)
Includes bibliographical references and index.
1. Churchill, Caryl – Criticism and interpretation. I. Title.
PR6053.H786Z78 2014
822'.914–dc23
2014023243

ISBN: 978-0-415-34577-4 (hbk)
ISBN: 978-0-415-34578-1 (pbk)
ISBN: 978-0-203-56730-2 (ebk)

Typeset in Sabon
by Taylor and Francis Books

For
Max Stafford-Clark
and
Tanya Gerstle
(the best actor trainer in the world)

Caryl Churchill is to contemporary theatre
what Picasso was to modern art.

Sarah Daniels

Contents

Illustrations

Acknowledgements

This book is based on more than 15 years of engagement with Churchill's work as a teacher, scholar, director and spectator. I have an enormous debt of gratitude to those in the Department of English at the University of York and to Vice-Chancellor Sir Ron Cooke. My thanks to Kenneth and Pat Dixon are beyond expression: they have unfailingly supported my work, and indeed supplied the theatre spaces in which I have been able to work and rehearse: they have followed the artistic careers of many of my collaborators. My deep gratitude also goes to Gordon and Francesca Horsfield and David and Linda Foster, who have always been supportive. Key enthusiasts and colleagues have been: Michael Cordner, Andy Tudor, Richard Rowland, Judith Buchanan, John Bowen, Derek Attridge, David Attwell, Jack and Judy Donovan, Jason Edwards, Dawn Fowler, Mark and Trish Jenner, Anna Harpin, Geoff Wall, Victoria Coulson, Simon Mills, Nik Miller, Peter Holland, Elizabeth Tyler, Sue Mendes, Varsha Panjwani and Trevor Sheldon. Deepest thanks to the York Theatre Royal for hosting my productions. Talia Rodgers and Ben Piggott at Routledge were always generous with their time and energy on this project.

My productions, and the research and writing of this book, have been supported by the AHRC, the University of York and the esteemed hat-makers of York College. University and conservatoire communities in Australia have been inspirational. I am indebted to Professor Peta Tait and the School of Communication, Arts and Critical Enquiry at Latrobe University where I was a visiting fellow. I was fortunate enough to be made inaugural visiting professor of performing arts at the School of Arts, Letters and Media at the University of Sydney in 2013 and owe much to that friendly and stimulating environment. My thanks go to Annamarie Jagose, Peter Marks, Vic Burrows, Eileen Corrigan, Paul O'Dwyer, Laura Ginters, and Amanda Card. Invaluable research and other assistance was undertaken by Eleanor Paremain, Janet McGaw and Virginia Hatton. The last draft of this book was written in John and Cynthia Gregory-Roberts's enchanted garden in Sydney – to them and to Ros Arnold my warm thanks. I am grateful for the help of the British Museum Library, the National Theatre Archive, the Lebrecht Archive, the Royal Court, and the Sheffield Crucible Theatre.

I have learned so much from interviews and conversations with professional actors and directors that the list of people to thank would be too vast to include here. Above all, I would like to thank Max Stafford-Clark, who has been tremendously indulgent with his time over the years. Howard Davies, Les Waters, Mark Wing-Davey, Sam West, Michael Billington and Baroness McIntosh also shared their thoughts in extremely helpful ways. Many thanks to Victoria Coulson for reading and commenting on early drafts of the first two sections. I owe much to Natsu Hattori who gave sensitive and insightful feedback and was a tremendous cheerleader. Emilie Morin cast a meticulous eye over *The Hospital at the Time of the Revolution* and gave advice on Algerian history. I am very grateful to Maggie Gale for her patience and her scrupulous reading of the manuscript.

Last but far from least are all the actors, assistant directors, musicians and choreographers who have worked with me and vastly enriched my interpretations of Churchill's work. Thanks especially to Kai Low, Paul Birch, Tom Cantrell, Lewis Charleston, Fiona Cooper, Panda Cox, Mark Edel Hunt, Marcus Emerton, Zita Farkas, Frances Flannery, Marin Hirschfeld, Sophie Larsmon, Tanith Lindon, Pete Mendham, Rebecca Morgan, Anna Rohde, Matt Springett, Alan Stewart, Jim Stephenson, Ellie Taylor and Ben Tyler-Wray. I was fortunate enough to work with choreographer Jordana Hill on *Far Away*; and for each Churchill production with the outstanding young filmmaker, Nikolaus Morris and with Paul Abbott who is, quite simply, a musical genius.

Chronology of Theatre Plays/ Dance Pieces/Librettos

Seagulls was written in 1978 but remains unperformed.
Hotel was subsequently renamed *Eight Rooms* and performed with *Two Nights*.
In 1999 Churchill directed Wallace Shawn's *Our Late Night*.
Student plays are not included in this list.

Note: This volume uses Churchill's collected editions of plays where
      possible.

Part I
Life and Politics

1 Contexts

Overview

Frequently described as 'the first dramatist of the 21st century'[1] and 'the most consistently innovative playwright of the postwar era' (Sierz 2011:25), Caryl Churchill is one of the most significant political dramatists in Western theatre. Her professional work reaches back to the 1960s and is significant for its continual demonstration of audacious experiment and its resistance to classification. Deemed 'unholy in her variability',[2] Churchill the artist is renowned for her unpredictable experiments and for her willingness to take risks. Alastair Macaulay declared her 'the most original playwright in Britain', and argued that she writes 'like a visionary, a poet, an absurdist, a politician, a satirist'.[3] An intellectual, a radical innovator, and a highly sophisticated formal craftswoman, she has always challenged mainstream cultural assumptions about theatre as an art form and commercial product, and is used to controversy. Her decision, for example, to publish *Seven Jewish Children* (2009) on the internet and to allow performances on the proviso that donations are collected for a Palestinian charity meant that she was able to effect political action through the very decision to produce her play. Since *Seven Jewish Children* may be performed by any group of people, anywhere (local censorship laws permitting), she also demolished the division between professional and amateur, and negated the necessity for particular kinds of traditional theatrical venue. In doing so, Churchill threw down the gauntlet to theatrical oligarchies – who found themselves suddenly extraneous to control and commodification. Let there be no doubt – this is an artist who both confounds and provokes.

Churchill's work shows a lifelong quest for new forms of non-naturalist political theatre: she cuts across and fuses artistic disciplines, and is as likely to work with musicians, composers, singers, choreographers and dancers as she is with actors and directors. Famously, she works from the premise that 'anything is possible in theatre'.[4] As she has said:

> I do enjoy the form of things. I enjoy finding a form that seems best to fit what I'm thinking about [...] I enjoy plays that are non-naturalistic and don't move at real time.
>
> (Kay 1989: 42)

Although long associated with the Royal Court Theatre, she is not in the dominant realist tradition that the Court has marketed hard. Churchill belongs to the same generation of playwrights as David Hare, Howard Brenton, David Edgar, Pam Gems and Trevor Griffiths, and it is the influences of pre-World War II surrealism and the post-war politics of absurdist drama (especially Eugène Ionesco) as well as the minimalism and gestural theatre of Samuel Beckett that continue to stand out in her work – from the early, chilling radio plays of the 1960s to later theatre works such as *Vinegar Tom*, *Fen*, *The Skriker*, *Mad Forest*, *Blue Heart*, *Dream Play* and *Far Away*. Reading or performing her work demands a facility to make sometimes fantastical leaps of imagination, and meaning is often layered. Who can forget the nightmarish gibberish of *The Skriker* and her murderous appetites? Who can forget the scene between the vampire and the painfully submissive, self-destructive dog in *Mad Forest*? Who does not shiver at the stuttering form of *Blue Heart*, which threatens to implode into the violent unspeakability of its incest narrative (notwithstanding the entrance of a ten-foot tall bird)? And yet the surrealism is presented in a down-to-earth fashion; it is woven into the fabric of the everyday with no self-consciousness. Internal and external worlds, the quotidian and the gothic, past and present are all in continual collision in Churchill's plays, and suggested by visual and sonic landscapes that often have echoes of a version of theatrical magic realism.

Churchill's more recent preoccupations reflect the new definitions of post-Thatcherite British political theatre offered by Amelia Howe Kritzer in a country where current political life 'is characterised by public disengagement and detachment' but theatre culture is still thriving, and arguably 'of renewed strength,' as playwrights dissect the individual's relationship to structures of power – whether the power of collectives, global organisations, technology, religions, nations, the media, knowledge flow or ethical codes (Kritzer 2008: 26, 221). Kritzer groups Churchill both with an older generation of political playwrights such as David Hare, David Edgar and Howard Brenton, and with later generations that include Tanika Gupta, Kwame Kwei-Armah, Sarah Kane, Gregory Burke and Simon Stephens (Kritzer 2008). The thematic agendas of Churchill's plays repeatedly address war, genocide, imperialism, capitalism and the global economy, environmental atrocity, sexuality, scientific knowledge, patriarchy, motherhood and the politics of reproduction, cruelty and violence, and parenting and child abuse. Her dramas mirror contemporary international preoccupations and offer an embedded scrutiny of the individual's relationship to the ideologies inherent within specific social and institutional structures. Western models of the family are often represented as a microcosm of economic and political environments, which are invariably darkly catastrophic. Home is not a safe place. It is a site of gothic collapse and psychic mayhem.

My own fascination with Churchill has come from my Brechtian training and commitment to a political theatre that is also poetic. I admire the ways in which Churchill has taken certain devices deployed by Brecht and advanced them further than he could have imagined. Churchill thrives on rehearsal processes, holds a lifelong admiration for actors, and has confessed to a susceptibility to 'falling in love with performers, with what I see them do to my plays'.[5] Her varied working processes and collaborations constitute important challenges to how we understand a theatrical event, what it might look like, how it might sound and where it takes place. My intrigue ensues from the plays I have directed and the many students I have taught, as well as a ghoulish interest in representing the apocalyptic. Churchill's work is a sustained exploration of the politics and operations of complicity, and although few remark on it, it shows an urgent engagement with the human rights of women and children. While it is unusual for academics to comment on the terrifying suggestibility of Churchill's landscapes, actors and directors know of the darkness and destruction her work confronts. Actress

Kathryn Hunter has spoken of inhabiting the Skriker, a part she felt was both compelling and cataclysmic, involving 'about thirteen different characters' and more to do with 'basic drives than psychological characterisations' (Oddey 2005: 177).

Churchill's worlds are the stuff of nightmare, of primal, post-Freudian horror, where children know no safety. Parents and step-parents consistently fail to nurture and protect; indeed, they abandon, torture, abuse, groom and openly threaten to kill their progeny. Often children have no voice in Churchill's plays – they are the ghosts occupying a strange no man's land, like the ragged, bare-footed boy in *Fen*; the mostly offstage Susy in *Blue Heart*, whose impending but endlessly deferred arrival suggests the unspeakable trauma of a dreadful family secret. They cannot speak or are denied speech because they are the purveyors of a truth that cannot be named – like Francoise in *The Hospital at the Time of the Revolution*, who is mentally scarred by the knowledge of her parents' complicity in the colonial regime; Angie in *Top Girls* faces a destitute future because she is failed by both carers and state welfare systems; in *A Number*, a psychopathic father reveals his delusional 'mercy' to the son whom he decided not to murder: 'I could have killed you and I didn't [...] I spared you though you were this disgusting thing' (*Plays 1* 1985: 197). In *Fen*, Churchill portrays the physical abuse of a child by her stepmother – one of the few contemporary onstage scenes of a child being tortured (*Plays 2* 1990: 153–54). Adult family members condemn their children to a violent future, and become bedtime propagandists and warmongers. There's nothing cosy about Churchill, just as there's nothing cuddly about Alfred Hitchcock, Roald Dahl, David Lynch or Tim Burton. Like the transformation of people into symbolic Nazis in Ionesco's play *Rhinoceros*, Churchill's nightmares are all the more chilling because they are based on political realities.

Anonymity and privacy

Born in 1938, Churchill has carefully eschewed the interface with the media and critical establishments sought by playwrights such as Harold Pinter and David Hare. Few official photographs are in circulation because Churchill prefers her reputation to rest on her work. This preference for media anonymity, in addition to the chameleonic nature of her writing career, has had an interesting impact on her reception history. The majority of academics have privileged a history of male playwrights over female in twentieth-century British theatre history, which standard academic texts reflect (see, for example, Shellard 1999; Eyre and Wright 2000; Innes 2002).

During her career she has given only limited interviews, mainly to women, and since the 1980s has not added to the sketchy details about her upbringing that she revealed early on. In the past decade, public appearances and platform events in Britain have been a rarity, and Max Stafford-Clark, a lifelong professional friend of Churchill's, has described her as 'notoriously reluctant to write or talk about her own writing' (Roberts and Stafford-Clark 2007: 88). In 2012 her long-time publisher, Nick Hern, revealed that she once implied that public self-analysis might disrupt her creativity: 'I really don't like talking about my work. It makes me self-conscious when I come to write the next thing.'[6] Like Beckett she is 'very wary' of labels (Itzin 1980: 279) and is positively uninterested in cultures of celebrity, once telling the hapless American critic Mel Gussow: 'I want to be either Homer or Anon, one of those people no one says anything about.' In the same meeting, Churchill helpfully suggested that Gussow fashion his article around her dislike of interviews, which he duly did.[7]

A writer of brilliant precision, Churchill is also exasperated by the reductiveness of descriptive vocabularies (Fitzsimmons 1989: 91). Critical terms have been attached to her that have suggested that her work is fixed and transparent, as if Churchill as writer, theatre-maker and intellectual does not evolve. In fact, she is a constant inventor and reinventor, or – to use Dominic Dromgoole's more sensational phrasing – 'a category smasher' (Dromgoole 2000: 52). She has been a keen reader of psychological and psychiatric discourses (among others), but since her early career has been quiet about her personal development. The details of her own life have been worked less overtly into her plays than many other writers and her artistic leanings are towards provocation. Churchill reacted antipathetically to the autobiographical writing embraced by female novelists of her generation in the 1960s and 1970s: 'That seemed to be something I definitely didn't want to do. I wanted to make something more distanced' (Cousin 1988: 5). While Churchill has displayed a linguistic range that includes hyper-real dialogue, voices from different historic periods, satiric verse, song lyrics, Joycean streams of consciousness and punning, as well as the evocatively poetic, she is also famously spare with her dialogue, many of her works indicating a profound fascination with the limitation of words and the eloquence of silence. The caution she exudes when trying to describe her creative processes is apparent to anyone who follows her appearances. If she wishes to make a political statement in public, she is more likely to do it through a letter to *The Guardian*. While her plays are profoundly engaged with anti-capitalist and anti-globalist agendas, Churchill herself has rarely sought the speaker's podium. In this book I make no apology for arguing that Churchill is one of the most significant political playwrights of our time.

Childhood and parental influence

Intensely private, Churchill has said little about her upbringing and there are few interview sources. An only child, she spent most of the first ten years of her life in London and, although a very young infant during World War II, she was evidently imbued with an alertness to the international political arena through her father's art. Robert Churchill was a cartoonist by profession and Churchill has recalled how 'I grew up with his cartoons of the war – of Goebbels and Mussolini', and explained how she came to understand that there was a link between her own career and her father's: 'Cartoons are really so much like plays. An image with somebody saying something' (Thurman 1982: 53). In political cartoons, word and image are often juxtaposed to create an explosive contextual clash. Such effects are apparent in many of Churchill's plays, and she has explicitly talked of a world of the grotesque borrowed from cartoon art, and the analogy between cartoons and her satiric caricatures, for example – of city financiers in *Serious Money*.[8]

From 1948 to 1955 the family was located in Montreal, Canada, where Churchill continued her schooling. Churchill has said little about her early creative life: only that she wrote short stories and poems, performed playlets for her parents, made up performances with friends, and spent one summer painting theatre sets when she was 15. She also developed an interest in going to see plays. (Cousin 1988: 3; Thurman 1982: 54). Churchill's mother left school at 14, worked as a secretary, and then became a fashion model, notably appearing in an advertisement for the well-known bedtime drink company Ovaltine, and landed a few 'bit parts in films' (Thurman 1982: 54). The little that Churchill has said indicates that she was intrigued by the transgressiveness of her mother going out to work in an industry not considered suitable for respectable married women.

> I mostly remember my mother at home, but she did talk to me about working, and the fact that she used not to wear her wedding ring to work. I had the feeling, rather early on, that having a career was in no way incompatible with staying married and being very happy.
>
> (Thurman 1982: 54)

Churchill's idealised perception of her mother's harmonisation of marriage and career was tested by the pain and unhappiness she herself endured when confined to the house caring for her children in the early years of her own married life. Although her father was the more sustainedly visible, professional working artist and Churchill drew inspiration from his craft, she was clearly also tantalised by the world of theatre mediated by her mother's interest in acting and fashion. It is also apparent that intergenerational tensions between mother and daughter eased when Churchill and her husband radically reorganised their domestic life in the early 1970s, enabling her to concentrate more fully on her career: 'My relationship with my mother has become so much better in the course of this whole period [...] because I became myself' (Thurman 1982: 57). Significantly, Churchill's plays have repeatedly interrogated parents' relationships with their children, and have been markedly invested in reflecting on motherhood and the ways in which mothers are devalued, and politically and socially scapegoated.

Artistic experiments at university

From 1957 to 1960 Churchill read for a BA in English at Lady Margaret Hall, Oxford University. Philosophically, she was strongly influenced by two schools of thought: Buddhism and Marxism (Thurman 1982: 54). Like many of her generation, Churchill's abhorrence of the political right stemmed from a childhood and adolescence freighted with the atrocities perpetrated by fascist dictatorships and imperialist regimes, and her engagement with Marxism during the 1960s, 1970s and 1980s must be contextualised in relation to those horrors. While Marxism aimed to provide an alternative to the socio-economic inequalities fostered by Western capitalism, Buddhism offered a non-violent philosophy, respect for the natural environment and promoted peace rather than war.

Churchill's theatrical writing was spurred by a friend and fellow student, who asked her to write a play that he could direct. She adapted one of her own short stories and *Downstairs* received a production at Oriel College, Oxford, in 1958 and was selected for performance at the National Union of Students/*Sunday Times* Drama Festival in 1959. From the first, then, Churchill stood out as a dramatist and found an intellectual and creative community at Oxford that stimulated her. Three further student productions followed: *Having a Wonderful Time*, at the Questors Theatre in 1960; *You've No Need to be Frightened*, a student radio drama in 1961; and *Easy Death*, at the Oxford Playhouse in 1961. These works are unpublished but limited summaries do exist (Randall 1988: 4–5; Fitzsimmons 1989: 12–13). For today's reader, *Downstairs* has echoes of Pinter's stage world in *The Room*, though it predates it: a mother feels threatened by her son's involvement with the family downstairs and tells him to end his relationship with their daughter Catherine. The son kills Catherine, and the mother feels they will be forever trapped by this act. *Having a Wonderful Time*, the clichéd formula still used by many on their postcards sent from foreign climes to provide a false performance of enjoyment for their loved ones, explores the relationship between Anne and three male admirers while she is on holiday in the south of France. Anne, conditioned as a 1950s middle-class woman not to believe in her abilities or the possibility of economic independence, chooses the relationship that will increasingly negate her and deprive her of autonomy. The radio play *You've No Need to be Frightened* investigates the destructive relationship between a husband and wife. Even here, one can see Churchill's anxiety about the potentially disastrous effects of domestic dependence and childbirth on a woman's self-esteem and creative ambition. *Easy Death*, an obvious precursor to *Owners* (1972), focuses on a meeting between a capitalist zealot and a radical anti-capitalist, which results in a death.

Having a Wonderful Time is written mainly in verse, and *Easy Death* uses both verse and song, as well as experiments with time shifts – all devices that Churchill has repeatedly deployed. Both latter plays reflect a preoccupation with the prescriptiveness of Western capitalism and its ideological imperative to create systems that coerce and condition its subjects to commit acts of self-harm or violence to others.

Ways of seeing: a theatre manifesto

the fifties seem to have been excited by discovering the working man in his kitchen and think he is enough in himself
(Churchill 1960: 458)

In her twenties, Churchill can best be understood as defining herself with and against a particular intellectual moment shaped strongly by the post-war 1950s. Her dramatic radicalism, critical acuity and activist frustration are all evident in the polemic 'Not Ordinary, Not Safe', printed in 1960 when Churchill was just 22. In this essay she launches a blistering attack on the contemporary drama then in vogue and prescribes some remedies of her own. With remarkable prescience, Churchill questions the agenda of John Osborne's *Look Back in Anger* (1956), the supposedly foundational moment of the post-war theatre myth expostulated by so many at the time. It is the only manifesto by Churchill in the public realm and in it she analyses the insular, regressive conservatism of a small group of privileged males controlling London's theatres, who insist on the supposedly 'natural' dominance of nineteenth-century forms of naturalism.

Churchill advocates an ambitious agenda of change. In her evangelism for new subjects and forms, her broadside is reminiscent of Brecht's call for theatrical revolution following World War I (Brecht 1964: 66–67), but she draws particular attention to the curiously unimaginative English response to non-realist modernist experiment. Angered by Osborne and the Royal Court, who inhabit what she calls 'the age of the small statement' (Churchill 1960: 445), Churchill exposes the lack of political and aesthetic ambition in English 1950s theatre, arguing that so-called 'kitchen sink' drama is anything but innovative:

the working-class intellectual cracking at his wife's caricatured Daddy is a stock character. We know the English are still snobbish about accents, we're not happy about the British Empire, suburban life is often dull and many middle-aged men are unfulfilled. We can't communicate with each other, have a lot of illusions and we don't know what if anything life is about. All right. Where do we go from here?

(Churchill 1960: 445)

Churchill characterises English theatre as constituted by 'depressing plays of the depressing fifties' (Churchill 1960: 445), nostalgic for a morally indefensible imperial past. Such plays, she argues, simply reinforce political failures already acknowledged without proposing charters for meaningful change. In *Look Back in Anger*, a supposedly state-of-the-nation play, Churchill points out that the protagonists, Jimmy Porter and Alison, are left stranded in their infantile delusions and sadomasochistic psychodrama. Deplorably, the misogyny of Porter's psychological and physical abuse of his wife goes unquestioned – indeed, it is even celebrated as a legitimate vehicle for his political frustration. In Pinter's *The Caretaker*, Aston can only stutter his way to final silence. In Arnold Wesker's *Roots*, an ideology of romantic love is offered as a sop to the failure of socialist idealism. Although, like their English counterparts, Churchill argues that Beckett and Ionesco present unhelpful dystopias, she apprehends the innovation of their linguistic and visual paradigms, and calls for a utopian quest to explore socialist agendas in ways that provoke change. English forms of naturalism are not inherently interrogatory as supposed, declares Churchill, and too many plays are 'small', 'safe', 'empty, repetitive and irritating' (Churchill 1960: 446–48), failing to fulfil what the artist's role must be – to provide alternative ways of seeing:

It's as if the playwright has a special prefabricated view of the world which he doesn't like so he goes round picking out loose stones with his penknife and writing rude words on the wall, instead of pulling the wall down, designing a better building – not designing a new society but finding a better, broader way of looking. [...] Let's widen our range, and without ignoring our problems get them into a different perspective. [...] Playwrights don't give answers, they ask questions. We need to find new questions, which may help us answer the old questions or make them unimportant, and this means new subjects and new forms.

(Churchill 1960: 445–46)

Churchill expresses both intense frustration and passionate engagement with theatrical questions. She demonstrates an impressive understanding of a wide range of playwrights, including Doris Lessing, Archibald Macleish, W.H. Auden, T.S. Eliot, Arthur Miller, William Shakespeare, Bernard Kops, Brendan Behan and John Arden. She also references Greek drama, Romantic poets, and critics such as Bernard Levin and Walter Kerr. For a 22-year-old writer, the essay is highly informed, especially when one takes into account that few, if any, contemporary playwrights would have been required reading at Oxford University. Her response to what she calls the 'thin myth of failure and illusion' (Churchill 1960: 447) is a plea for forms that move away from the kind of slice-of-life, expositional naturalism promoted by the Royal Court, but 'not at the expense of the accurate observation of motive and conflicts' found in them (Churchill 1960: 448). Form and language should be experimental and visual stage worlds challenging; playwrights should seek compression of plot, a variety of rhythms, juxtapositions of song, prose and poetry, a spectrum of emotional moods and the cumulative effects of powerful stage pictures. What is said and how it is said are inseparable in theatre, Churchill argues: 'We overwork two aspects of language at the expense of the rest: the mechanical facts to be conveyed and the way people really talk' (Churchill 1960: 450). Greater technical and subject range are integral to one another and must be striven for, she continues. Above all, drama is an inherently communal art-form and offers the powerful potential 'of reaching people of every kind, developing a common culture and an awareness of how we act' (Churchill 1960: 451). There must be, reflects Churchill, ways of finding 'a good balance between life and art in contemporary drama' (Churchill 1960: 450). 'Not Ordinary, Not Safe' is a statement of commitment: it offers a fascinating project outline of the experiments and investigations that Churchill has pursued for the whole of her creative life.

Domestic politics

In 1961 Caryl Churchill married the progressive barrister David
Harter and was signed up by London's most celebrated, idiosyn-
cratic literary agent, Peggy Ramsay, following an introduction by
fellow undergraduate and burgeoning playwright John McGrath
(Chambers 1997: 268). McGrath was in tune with Churchill's politics and later became renowned for reinventing Brechtian form for a
socialist Scottish theatre. Between 1963 and 1969 Churchill gave
birth to three sons, and has alluded to the period up to 1972 as a
time of intense stress and emotional upheaval. During this time she
also suffered an unspecified number of miscarriages (Itzin 1980:
282). Despite the grave difficulties, not least in finding time and
energy to write, Churchill began her professional writing career in
the 1960s with the production of three radio plays: *The Ants* (1962),
Lovesick (1966) and *Identical Twins* (1968). The support of Peggy
Ramsay was paramount and her enterprise has been described as
'the most potent and influential play agency the theatrical world has
ever seen' (Chambers 1997: 3). Ramsay worried about selling
Churchill's politically experimental work, but facilitated the vital
professional contact at BBC Radio, John Tydeman, who went on to
direct all but one of Churchill's early radio plays. Ramsay also
negotiated Churchill's entrance to the Royal Court (via Oscar
Lewenstein). Churchill depended on Ramsay's personal support as
much as her business acumen:

> I had wanted to be a writer since I was a child but it was Peggy
> who made me feel that the theatre and writing plays are won-
> derful and worthwhile and that I could do it, that I should do it
> from the deepest part of myself. [...] It was her values that
> were important, and having her behind me, someone who you
> trust saying it's worth proceeding. It kept me going.
>
> (Chambers 1997: 272)

At this early stage of her professional career, Churchill was socially
marooned as a young wife and mother as well as psychologically
and physically very taxed:

> I felt isolated. I had small children and was having mis-
> carriages. It was an extremely solitary life. What politicised me

was being discontented with my own way of life − of being a
barrister's wife and just being at home with small children.

(Itzin 1980: 279)

Her plays at this time were more driven by a need for an emotional
outlet than work after 1972. Ramsay was Churchill's vital voice of
encouragement until her death in 1991.

Second wave feminism

By the early 1970s Churchill had discovered second wave feminism,
in the form of ground-breaking works such as Kate Millett's *Sexual
Politics* (1969), Eva Figes' *Patriarchal Attitudes* (1970) and Germaine Greer's *The Female Eunuch* (1970). She also discovered solidarity and community with women both in terms of protest and
making art (Aston 2001: 25). The impact of second wave feminism
reinforced Churchill's privately held views, but also encouraged her
to change her life. In 1972 there was certainly a revolution of
domestic sexual politics: following their decision to stop having
children (Churchill's husband underwent a vasectomy), and the
couple also took action on the division of labour, Churchill's husband handing in his notice to a private law firm to take on more
legal-aid cases. Changes in their life at home were also framed by
an increasing discomfort with professional working practices − as
Churchill has reported it: 'we didn't want to shore up a capitalist
system we didn't like' (Itzin 1980: 279). This change in working
arrangements was initiated by a complete break with their life in
London, and the family spent three months in Africa, followed by
three months on Dartmoor, where Churchill wrote *Objections to
Sex and Violence* (1975). It was payback time and Churchill
demanded dues from her husband: she had devoted her time to
'coping with things so that he could work for ten years, so why
didn't he take off time to do what I wanted?' (Itzin 1980: 279).

This decision to make a radical change in married and working
life reflected a growing chorus of Western feminist voices in the
1970s urging women to challenge their positions of economic, social
and sexual servitude. Churchill has referred to 1972 as a 'watershed', and argued that from this point on her life as a working
professional and as a mother became viable in an entirely new way

(Thurman 1982: 54). Clearly, given Churchill's productivity and success, she has astutely negotiated competing roles. Churchill was not an abstract feminist but, like many women of her era, experienced injustices before she found discourses that articulated them: if the mantra for 1970s feminists was that the personal was political there were good reasons that politicisation began in the domestic sphere and focused on sexual and reproductive issues. Churchill's plays abound with children under threat, dead or psychologically dying infants, and this may have a connection with her own miscarried children. Certainly, the relationship between the micro-politics of interpersonal relationships in a local setting, with the macro-politics of the state and global organisations is a notable feature in many of her plays.

Churchill and British theatre history

So far there are ten volumes dedicated to critiquing Churchill's plays: Aston (2001), Cousin (1989), Kritzer (1991), Randall (1988), Rabillard (1998), Tycer (2008), Roberts (2008), Aston and Diamond (2009), Adiseshiah (2009) and Gobert (2014). Fitzsimmons' *File on Churchill* (1989) provides useful primary and secondary source material on her early career. The vast majority of scholarship on Churchill's plays is in the form of articles, and the most influential are by Aston, Diamond, Kritzer and Reinelt. Her work since 1990 has received less detailed appraisal than her earlier work. Apart from Roberts' book, all the volumes mentioned above were written by female academics, which also gives pause for reflection.

There have been a number of obstructive features in the development of Churchill criticism. The odd distortions inherent in the dominant narrative of twentieth-century British theatre history, which since 1956 has privileged realism, maleness, and the Royal Court in relation to new theatre writing, still have powerful sway (Sierz 2011). Although she was a resident dramatist at the Royal Court, indeed the first woman writer appointed in that theatre's history, Churchill does not 'fit' the Court's post-1945 mythology of itself as a theatre that celebrates and promotes forms of realism – a tradition with which David Hare, for example, wholly identifies. Churchill's plays resist categorisation, each is quite unlike the last.[9] Dominic Dromgoole responds as do most directors to Churchill:

'The degree of innovation is extraordinary. Every play almost reinvents the form of theatre.'[10] There are theatre critics, however, who have criticised her precisely because of her startling originality.[11] Similarly, privileged narratives of the National Theatre and the Royal Shakespeare Company also pose a problem: Churchill has had little work staged there, and the conservatism of those institutions has not easily suited her radicalism. Churchill's works have been performed in amateur dramatic venues, school halls, student theatres, avant-garde studios, fringe theatres, dance studios, art galleries, subsidised theatres, the West End, Broadway and sundry international festivals all over the world but, until comparatively recently, British theatre historians have treated certain venues (the Royal Court, the Barbican and theatres at Stratford-on-Avon (RSC), and the National Theatre) as though they were all that 'British theatre' had to offer.

A further problem has been tokenism. Too many theatre historians have failed to look at matters afresh, and simply repeat the usual fictions. The peculiar myth that there were no or very few notable women playwrights before the 1960s is still depressingly pervasive. Feminist historians have, not surprisingly, proved quite the opposite (Gale 2002). For Chambers to argue that Churchill had 'no female playwrights as role models' is bizarre (Chambers 1997: 269). Thus Caryl Churchill and Sarah Kane have been bundled into recent twentieth-century histories as the token examples of successful female playwrights for reasons that have more to do with political correctness than with a desire to analyse their work seriously (Innes 2002; Eyre and Wright 2000).

Essentialist critiques have also been damaging in standard theatre histories. Christopher Innes' assertion that Churchill's dramatic structures are a mixture of essential maleness and essential femaleness – 'radical and dynamic' (by Innes' implication male) and his argument that 'as with other women playwrights, her [Churchill's] intuitive and fluid shaping of character and action reflects a specifically female consciousness' (Innes 2002: 512) – are patronising and reductive. As Kritzer highlights, Churchill also suffered from flawed analysis that separated the aesthetic from the political in her work (Kritzer 1991: 2). Typical of this approach was Innes, again, who polarised the 'poetic' and the 'political', assuming a mutual exclusivity and was therefore unable, for example, to marry the subject matter of *Serious Money* (1987) – the stock market and global capitalism – with the fact that the play is written in rhyming verse. Selecting form is a politically inflected decision, as Churchill argued in her manifesto essay, and there is no decree that the only style of political drama must be realist.

Lastly, there has been a tendency to deploy Churchill as *the* British example of a feminist playwright, and to burden her with the task of representing women's lives and women's issues in Britain. Male playwrights carry no such burden (unless they are writing from a minority subject position), and this pigeonholing, in part, accounts for the greater silence about her work from 1990 onwards, in which she has pushed experimental agendas much further.

Feminist critical perspectives

From the 1970s to the mid-1990s the frames most applied to Churchill's work were second wave feminist. But her work since 2000 does not so obviously lend itself to feminist analysis. During the 1980s and 1990s, Churchill became 'the great icon of second wave feminism in the British theatre': her plays *Cloud Nine*, *Top Girls*, *Vinegar Tom*, *Fen* and *Serious Money* serving as defining texts for the interrogation of feminist performance and its meanings. Indeed, for Janelle Reinelt, 'Churchill has stimulated and provoked some of the most important feminist thinking about the theatre since coming to critical attention in the mid-1970s' (Aston and Reinelt 2000: 174).

For feminist theatre critics such as Sue-Ellen Case, Elin Diamond and Elaine Aston, Churchill was a leading progenitor of what Case called 'the new poetics' in her celebrated book *Feminism and Theatre* (Case 1988: 132). Churchill's experiments with dramatic form and her interdisciplinary interest in mixing music, dance and theatre were seen to represent the advent of women as subjects as opposed to invisible objects of oppression. Her rebuttal of naturalist linearity, her adoption of the surreal and fantastic and her collaborations with feminist theatre collectives, were understood by second wave feminists as a necessary challenge to what they saw as inherently patriarchal and capitalist modes of realist performance-making. Churchill's interest in subverting the conventional politics of representation, her interrogation of modes of perception, and her innovations in usage of language and form seemed to present a utopia of myriad possibilities. 'The stage can be prepared for the entrance of the female subject,' declared Case, 'a new kind of revolution' was within reach 'for in the late twentieth century the mode of production which is central to the oppression of so many peoples lies within the ghettoes of signs and codes' (Case 1988: 132).

French feminist discourses developed by Hélène Cixous, Luce Irigaray and Julia Kristeva in the 1980s and 1990s focused on the body as the site of artistic creation and posited that it was possible for female artists to develop specifically feminine languages and forms. Known as *écriture féminine* or 'writing the body' and based on psychoanalytic ideas, these models came to be viewed as essentialist, and British and American feminist critics did not find that they adapted well to Churchill's clear interest in material production, social relations and structures of representation. Judith Butler's theorisations of performativity and the body in *Gender Trouble* and *Bodies that Matter* published in 1990 and 1993 respectively, proved more fruitful because Butler's argument that gender is continually constructed and performed seemed to lend itself neatly to theatrical practices, as I discuss later.

But it was Elin Diamond's essay 'Brechtian Theory/Feminist Theory' published in 1988 (see Martin 1996: 120–35) and later her book *Unmaking Mimesis* (1997) that investigated ways of applying Brechtian theory to feminist practice and prompted illuminating analyses about the political importance of Churchill's work. Inspired by Teresa de Lauretis' *Alice Doesn't* (1984) and *Technologies of Gender* (1987) and also by Laura Mulvey's seminal essay 'Visual Pleasure and Narrative Cinema' (1975), Diamond drew on Mulvey's notion of the male gaze and her contention that in Hollywood films the camera assumes the viewpoint of a male spectator, thereby fetishising the female performer. De Lauretis posed the problem of a doubled vision for feminist theorists; the problem of both recognising the representation of 'Woman' in cultural discourses and art works while simultaneously knowing that it is a false construct. Diamond argued for an intertextual reading of Brechtian and feminist theory, asserting that this could effect 'a recovery of the radical potential of Brechtian critique and a discovery, for feminist theory, of the specificity of theatre' (Martin 1996: 120). Brecht's demystification of the structures of representation was integral to his play scripts and to his processes of production, including his practices of acting, directing, visual and sound design. The Brechtian spectator's gaze is interrupted by alienation effects that provide a doubled focus, demonstrating to the viewer that a role can be distinguished as something distinct from the actor playing it. This Brechtian intervention, according to Diamond, 'signals a way of dismantling the gaze,' and can offer 'a female body in representation that resists fetishisation' as well as 'a viable position for the female spectator' (Martin 1996: 121). Together, Brechtian and feminist discourses and their application in the practice of theatre could provide a means of exposing the operations of 'an apparatus of representation with enormous formal political resonance' (Martin 1996: 122). Diamond cites Churchill's *Cloud Nine* as an example of the use of Brechtian distancing devices, in particularly cross-dressing, to generate a critique of men and women's social and sexual roles. Churchill's dramaturgy works, it is argued, to expose the cultural assumptions we make in relation to ideologies of gender:

> When spectators 'see' gender they are seeing (and reproducing) the cultural signs of gender, and by implication, the gender ideology of a culture. Gender in fact provides a perfect illustration of ideology at work since 'feminine' or 'masculine' behaviour usually appears to be a 'natural' – and thus fixed and unalterable – extension of biological sex. [...] When gender is alienated or foregrounded, the spectator is enabled to see a sign system *as* a sign system – the appearance, words, gestures, ideas, attitudes etc., that comprise the gender lexicon become so many illusionistic trappings to be put on or shed at will.
>
> (Martin 1996: 123)

Many of Churchill's plays deploy alienation devices in order to expose ideological oppression and injustice. Diamond also posits that the use of Brecht's theory of *Gestus* (historicisation coupled with the 'not, but' and alienation devices) by feminist playwrights and theorists could codify a new theatre-specific feminist language of analysis that she calls 'gestic criticism' (Martin 1996: 122). The Brechtian 'not, but' is a formulation to describe an action that signifies a set of possible actions beyond itself, and points towards alternative decisions and routes not taken. In other words, the 'not, but' device contains the elements that contain the seeds of an action's own deconstruction. Historicisation refers to the deliberate, self-reflexive creation of two realities – the past timeframe (an action that has occurred) and the present timeframe for performer and spectator (an action that the actor narrates and demonstrates in a way which causes the spectator to deliberate on the alternative actions). There are moments in many of Churchill's plays where this idea illuminates and, fascinatingly, there are also other moments when she subverts a Brechtian model for more powerful effect.

Brecht's and Diamond's theories are expressly utopian. Over the years, Churchill has become an increasingly dystopian writer, still interested in exposing many-sided complications to problems, but depicting cultures of denial and violence as enculturated phenomena without solution. In plays such as *Far Away* she suggests that humans are bent on a path of ecological catastrophe and self-destruction, enlisting their children to the same end disaster. In her plays of the 1990s and onwards, Churchill has increasingly deprived the spectator of conventional historical and narrative information, which can be read as her response to the features of globalised economies. In *This is a Chair* (1997) Churchill deploys Brechtian scene-headings that pointedly fail to provide the expected narrative lens but instead act as sensational framings for the apparently everyday scenes that follow. The juxtaposition of the scene headings with the content that follows, suggests we are watching actions that relate to complex political moments which have occurred on the world stage. Those very juxtapositions disrupt the spectator's viewing and force certain questions. To what extent is our view of the external world conditioned by information flow from the media? Given the incessant flow of data, what do we culturally prioritise and why? What is the nature of the intersection between quotidian scenes containing small, individual decisions with more ominous grand narrative politics? Churchill's world encodes a more technologically sophisticated world than Brecht's, and suggests that global economies, and global communications and weapons technology have changed the individual's relationship to the everyday. *This is a Chair* is just one example of the way Churchill has borrowed a Brechtian technique, extended and modified it. She is, unquestionably, as Reinelt has argued, 'one of Brecht's successors' and Reinelt is right to urge examination of both the Brechtian legacy (epic structures, character strategies, juxtaposition, montage and historicisation) in Churchill's work and her transcendence of it (Reinelt 1994: 107).

Diamond's overarching thesis in *Unmaking Mimesis* is an insightful way of analysing Churchill's work since the 1990s in relation to her modifications of Brechtian techniques, postmodern feminism, and is also a productive way of thinking about Churchill's continual experiments with form, the increasing textual minimalism of her work, and her preoccupation with song, music and languages of the body. Diamond argues that Churchill's plays 'have become increasingly attentive to the ideological nature of the seeable' (Diamond 1997: 85). Churchill's lighted stage 'queries the world of *permissible* visibility': 'specifically, the mystification of the body in representation has come to serve as a metaphor for the concealment of human, and especially female, experience under patriarchy and capitalism' (Diamond 1997: 85). Churchill complicates this analysis further because, in many of her plays, women are the instruments of other women's and children's oppression: her plays represented from the first what many feminist theorists acknowledged much later – that women are complicit in capitalist structures and can abuse their power just as much as men.

'Permissible visibility' is a useful concept to apply to Churchill's scopic project. In Act I of *Far Away* (2000) an adult female persuades a female child that she has not inadvertently witnessed anything criminal or sinister but has simply caught her uncle 'helping' people. In fact, it becomes apparent that the child has witnessed the forced removal of 'people' from their homes and that her carers are enablers in a genocide. The creeping horror of the scene is conveyed through the child's ignorance about the nature of the events she is reporting and her description of the amount of blood and the violence she saw. The child is eventually persuaded to do a good turn and help her aunt with the clean-up next day: she will literally have blood on her hands. The spectator is left to imagine what abominations may be happening a few yards from the child's bedroom and the numbers involved. In a later scene, Churchill minimalistically describes the action for the most shocking moment in the play, a grotesque dance of death performed by the condemned, who are chained, abject and on their way to execution, forced to parade in surreal hats that have been framed as works of art made for the discerning consumer. This is the only time we see the dark world of the condemned (who are both male and female) and we never hear their stories but we 'know' their fate without having to see it. Churchill's 'permissible visibility' reflects the enforced silence and invisibility of the victims of torture, dictatorship and genocide which crowd our newspapers and screens and yet remain marginal. In *Seven Jewish Children* (2009), it is significant that we never see the female child locked away for her own protection and that we never hear her speak: in a sense, she is in limbo, one of the living dead. This instance is an interesting take on what Diamond describes as Churchill's feminist project – 'no ecstatic "writing the body" but rather a foregrounding of the apparatus that makes the writing impossible' (Diamond 1997: 85). It is telling that *Far Away* and *Seven Jewish Children* feature girls and suggests that Churchill still believes that girls suffer greater oppression than boys. For Diamond, Churchill's work 'fully belongs in the postmodern moment' and is 'almost unique in attempting to represent multinational capitalism's effect on women' (Diamond 1997: 104). But the utopianism of Diamond's Brecht essay of 1988 has slipped away: she argues not that Churchill's theatre can effect change but rather that she has predicted it: 'It is impossible to see her plays and not feel that irreversible changes in economic production have altered traditional social and symbolic structures' (Diamond 1997: 104).

In the 1990s postcolonial theory and work inspired by Homi Bhabha and Gayatri Chakravorty Spivak collided with white, Western schools of feminist theory, which were attacked for their Anglo-American, First World bias and for privileging sexuality and gender over race and class. Aston and Case have provided a compelling account of how the International Federation for Theatre Research's feminist research working group has redefined itself since 1994 and re-thought its working practices to ensure cross-cultural, local and global debate between developing world and developed world scholars (Aston and Case 2007: 1–6). Transnational, cosmopolitic, diaspora and applied theatre frames have fast emerged in the past ten years and all have informed feminist theatre practice but there is still much to be addressed, including theories of reception history that might allow for differing cultural receptions of the same play (see *Top Girls* and *A Number*). In this sense, Churchill's work too reflects its author's second wave origins and this has led to certain problems as I outline later in my discussion of *Cloud*

Nine. Despite these problems Aston and Case specifically assert that Churchill's work comprises an important part of international feminist performance practice and scholarship (Aston and Case 2007: 4). Judging from the emerging testimony of scholars, practitioners and spectators in developing countries or from those living in oppressive regimes or in countries of economic deprivation, productions of Churchill's plays still form part of strategies for resisting political marginalisation and pressing for political change.

In the twenty-first century, second wave theorists have increasingly expressed their dismay at the appearance of the notion of 'post-feminism' (which is often conflated with third wave or postmodern feminism). Authors Katie Roiphe and Natasha Walter are part of a generation who argue that feminism is outdated and redundant, celebrates victimisation, is in itself oppressive – and, in any case, has failed to unite women. Such opinions come across as narcissist and neo-liberal and seem to dismiss the global issues pertaining to women's rights, but they also suggest the successful hijacking of the term 'feminist' by right-wing factions who have contaminated the word with a myth of man-hating separatism. Aston and Harris' book *Feminist Futures?* poses the question of whether feminist communities across the world can re-form into a global mobilising force (Aston and Harris 2006: 1–15). In 2013 the signs are that women are uniting over women's rights agendas, and particularly to protest about violence and oppression at home and at work: the horrific rape and subsequent death of a young Indian woman in Delhi in December 2012 spawned mass protests and continued demands for changes in legislation; Julia Gillard, the former prime minister of Australia, was applauded for her impassioned battle against the misogyny of her male colleagues; the MP Stella Creasy became a national crusader against online misogyny and threats of violence against women; and Bridget Christie, a feminist comedian with an explicitly hard-hitting feminist show, won the Foster's Comedy Award at the Edinburgh Festival (only the second female ever to win it). We seem to be entering the fourth wave of feminism.

As this book makes clear, other frames besides the feminist illuminate Churchill's work: science, ethics, war, terror, climate change and masculinity – are all inscribed in her drama. But as a playwright, Churchill's significance to the development of feminist political theatre is unmatched.

Notes

1 John Peter, *Sunday Times*, 6 October 2002.
2 Ben Brantley, *New York Times*, 8 December 2004.
3 Alastair Macaulay, *Financial Times*, 4 December 2000.
4 Renate Klett, 'A Portrait of Caryl Churchill', *Theater Heute*, January 1984, p.19.
5 Judith Mackrell, *The Guardian*, 20 January 1994.
6 Mark Lawson, *The Guardian*, 3 October 2012.
7 Mel Gussow, *New York Times*, 22 November 1987.
8 J. Kay, *New Statesman and Society*, 21 April 1989.
9 Dan Rebellato (1999) argues that Churchill slips between social realist and 'formally experimental' traditions at the Royal Court, but the reading of a history of 'British drama' through one institution remains a problem. See also Aston and Diamond (2009: 166).
10 Mark Lawson, *The Guardian*, 3 October 2012.
11 Walter Kerr, *New York Times*, 12 June 1983.

Part II

Early Plays and Collaborations, the 1960s–1970s

2 Transformations: The Long 1960s

Popular protest

The political and social contexts in which Churchill began her professional writing career significantly informed her work. The international scene was tumultuous: terrorist activities and conflicts loomed large in the news headlines. The ideological divide between the communist East and the capitalist West was unforgettably symbolised through the erection of the Berlin Wall in 1961, and the Cuban Missile Crisis of 1962 exacerbated the so-called Cold War still further. After a bitter eight-year war with France, Algerians finally gained independence in 1962, their struggle and victory bringing about more reflection on the iniquities of imperialism. But it was the assassinations of the reformist American president John F. Kennedy in 1963, and of the charismatic black activist Martin Luther King in 1968 that really highlighted the West's continuing oppression of ethnic minorities. International student protests in 1968 came to emblematise the 1960s: May 1968 in Paris, in particular, encapsulated utopian beliefs that popular protest could effect significant changes and even bring down governments. Those protests might have failed in their immediate objectives but they characterised the 1960s as an era in which the opinions of ordinary citizens were expressed on the streets and *en masse*.

In his absorbing book *The Sixties*, Arthur Marwick describes the period between 1958 and 1974, 'the long sixties,' as a revolution in terms of a 'transformation in lifestyles, family relationships, and personal freedoms for the vast majority of ordinary people' (Marwick 1998: 7, 15). Broadly speaking, the 1960s are noted for the rise of new subcultures and protest groups that were set up in opposition to dominant state structures and ideologies. Marxism provided campaign frameworks for new leftist, anti-capitalist movements that fought for changes in legislative policy across a wide spectrum of issues, ranging from anti-war agendas to civil rights, women's rights, gay rights, child poverty and environmental protection (Nicholson 2012).

Although Harold Macmillan, the Conservative prime minister in 1960, famously spoke of 'the winds of change' that had brought an end to the British Empire and presaged the demise of imperialism in South Africa, he cannot have imagined the extent of the changes in domestic policy that were effected over the next 15 years (mainly under Harold Wilson's Labour Government from 1964 to 1970). A selective list of legislation voted through the British Parliament gives some idea of the legacy: in 1961 suicide was decriminalised; in 1965 capital punishment was abolished; in 1967 the Abortion Act legalised termination and the National Health Service (Family Planning) Act was passed; the Sexual Offences Act of 1967 legalised homosexual acts between consenting adults; in 1968 theatre censorship was abolished, which had been in operation since Elizabeth I's reign in the sixteenth century; in 1969 the voting age was lowered from 21 to 18; the Divorce Reform Act of 1969 made divorce more accessible; and the Equal Pay Act of 1970 offered legal protection to women and ethnic minorities from discrimination at work. Churchill may have been housebound and felt removed from public events in the early years of her marriage, but intellectually she belonged to the committed, Marx-inspired progressives of her day, and her work from this time is intricately bound up with major agendas of the era.

Younger British citizens, especially the university-educated, had a sense that they belonged to what the fiction writer Angela Carter called 'an unprecedented and exponentially expanding, full-blooded, enquiring rootless urban intelligentsia', which could cross social boundaries in a country that had been 'brutally disfigured' by the class system (Maitland 1988: 210–12). Like many other contemporaries of Churchill, Carter experienced a greater social mobility; a relaxation of sexual mores and the revolution of 'more or less 100 per cent effective methods of birth control' (Maitland 1988: 214); a more pervasive sense of internationalism spurred by a new intensity of cultural exchange, especially in fashion, music, film and television; and a greater awareness of other European cultures – symbolised by Britain's entry into the European Union in 1973. Julie Christie, an iconic actress of the 1960s, reinforces Carter's views:

> There was a real consciousness about the state of the world [...] because the culture of the sixties was fundamentally anti-capitalist, anti-multinationalist. And with that real internationalism came the beginning of an ecological awareness [...]. There was a powerful sense of something new happening, of excitement, and breakthrough and danger.
>
> (Maitland 1988: 170–72)

Carter has vivid recollections of the international demonstrations against the Vietnam War, fought from 1962 to 1974, during which America engaged in a brutal ideologically driven killing spree, notoriously using napalm and other toxic substances, to back a corrupt regime in South Vietnam against communist North Vietnam and the communist Vietcong. She gives an evocative description of why the Vietnam War had such extraordinary meaning for her generation:

> Towards the end of the sixties one felt one was living on the edge of the unimaginable; there was a constant sense of fear and excitement and, of course, it was to do with war. Wars are great catalysts for social change and even though it was not *our* war, the Vietnam war was a conflict between the First and Third World, between Whites and non-Whites and, increasingly, between the American people, or a statistically significant percentage thereof, and Yankee imperialism. And the people won. Whatever happened afterwards, however much they rewrite that war and whatever else the US does, it was the first war in the history of the world where the boys were brought back from the front due to popular demand from their own side.
>
> (Maitland 1988: 212)

Churchill's experience of the 1960s was one of childbearing and domestic confinement: a story just as familiar as Carter's and Christie's narratives of excitement, activism and sexual abandon. Given the contexts of the 1960s it is not surprising that Churchill's plays consistently demonstrated the interrelatedness of family and interpersonal power dynamics with capitalist superstructures, war and imperialism.

Radio plays: selves and others

Churchill's professional career began in radio, a medium to which she was well accustomed and it proved formative in developing her ear for soundscapes. Radio offered her a more accessible market than theatre at a moment immediately preceding the proliferation of fringe theatres and experimental companies in the late 1960s and 1970s, and her writing for radio was done entirely at home between births, miscarriages and childrearing (Thurman 1982: 54). Her radio director at the time, John Tydeman, recalls her speaking of 'writing at the kitchen table with her sons around her'.[1] As Churchill has explained:

> As a child I was of a generation who grew up with radio, not television. Radio was nice because you could do other things at the same time, like drawing. I went on listening to radio, Beckett plays, for example until, I suppose, my early twenties. Radio was really quite important to me.
>
> (Cousin 1988: 3–4)

The influence of both Beckett and Pinter resonates strongly in her work for radio, but Churchill creates mesmerising and uniquely disturbing interior worlds and word scores. The radio plays have been given scant attention but there is no question, even at this stage, that Churchill was a brilliant innovator. For Geraldine Cousin these plays should not simply be viewed as 'a form of apprenticeship' but as 'amongst the most powerful and moving' examples of her work (Cousin 1989: 80). Churchill once described her early plays as manifesting two obsessions: one with interior worlds or 'mental states', as she phrased it, and the other with anti-capitalism (Thurman 1982: 54). It is interesting to note that Churchill was highly independent as an emerging artist and determined to develop her own radio experiments: she did not seek any payment or commissions in advance, which was unusual, as Tydeman has reported:

We never commissioned her. Even with a work that had taken a great deal of historical research, such as one called *Schreber's Nervous Illness*, the play would just turn up in the post.[2]

Churchill's first professional play, *The Ants*, was broadcast in 1962. In it a young boy, Tim, is caught up in his parents' destructive divorce proceedings and successively failed by all three of the adults entrusted with his care – his mother, father and grandfather. His fixation with an ant colony turns from benevolent curiosity to outright destruction and, encouraged by his grandfather, he pours petrol on it, the play ending with an explosive holocaust, Tim's laughter and the eerie crashing of the sea. The domestic war between the parents is mirrored by what Churchill has made clear is the real focus of this play – news of actual war and the dropping of a devastating bomb (Thurman 1982: 54). These external details suggest historical resonances with Nazi atrocities and with the nuclear annihilation of Hiroshima by the Americans, and for listeners at the time the Algerian War of Independence was still fresh. Tim's domestic conditioning to exert authority through violence is carefully connected to his potential to become a future killing-machine.

All the radio plays depict characters in states of disturbance, but *Lovesick* (1966) and *Schreber's Nervous Illness* (1972) are explicitly concerned with psychiatric discourses. Churchill's interest in deconstructing traditional, mechanistic approaches to the treatment of the mentally ill was stimulated by the intellectual controversy generated by the writings of psychiatrist R.D. Laing throughout the 1960s. Laing was the first of the eclectic British existential school of psychotherapy and his book, *The Divided Self: An Existential Study in Sanity and Madness* (1960) not only challenged and complicated the rigid cartographies of what 'madness', and quite specifically schizophrenia, might be, it also demystified the sufferers and suggested that modern western culture, and indeed psychiatry itself, inherently aggravated insanity. Laing's crusade 'to make madness, and the process of going mad, comprehensible' (Laing 1965: 9), along with his argument that traditional forms of psychiatric intervention were both ineffective and inhumane, had a profound impact on both professional and popular debates. *The Divided Self* became 'one of the most influential books of the sixties' (Maitland 1988: 215), and the author's utopian objective of releasing patients from the totalitarianism of conventional psychiatry and social prejudice was understood as an enlightenment project that, by extension, diagnosed capitalist society as a major cause of mental illness.[3] Laing's preface to the Pelican edition is a classic of 1960s' manifesto rhetoric, and it encapsulates the ideas of anti-authoritarianism, individual self-realisation and autonomy that obsessed so many intellectuals and artists of the time.

> Psychiatry could be, and some psychiatrists are, on the side of transcendence, of genuine freedom, and of true human growth. But psychiatry can so easily be a technique of brainwashing, of inducing behaviour that is adjusted, by (preferably) non-injurious torture. In the best places, where straitjackets are abolished, doors are unlocked, leucotomies largely forgone, these can be replaced by more subtle lobotomies and tranquillizers that place the bars of Bedlam and the locked doors *inside* the patient. Thus I would wish to emphasise that our 'normal' 'adjusted' state is too often the abdication of ecstasy, the betrayal of our true potentialities, that many of us are only too successful in acquiring a false self to adapt to false realities.
>
> (Laing 1965: 12)

Churchill's construction of the psychiatrist in *Lovesick* is an extreme manifestation of everything Laing abhorred about the violation that he thought much conventional medical practice condoned. Hodge is a chilling send-up of the then prevalent psychiatric belief in aversion therapy, often used to 'cure' homosexuality and other behaviours deemed 'unnatural'. A grotesquely deluded sociopath, Hodge pathologises sexual desire in himself and others, and treats it with a punitive drug regime. His reductive behaviourism inclines him to diagnose any human being he encounters as a formulaic psychiatric case and in the course of the play his patients are revealed to be far more self-aware and altogether less psychotic than he is. Hodge's 'work', which either backfires spectacularly or leaves his victims zombified, is repeatedly mocked and dismissed by other characters as 'downright immoral' (*Shorts* 1990: 5).

Hodge is exposed through his own narration of his interior life, which is interspersed with his interactions with others. This is a

clever device because, although the self-narration represents him as
pathologically suspicious and controlling, it is framed against the
apparent normality of his external persona. The listener's privileged access to Hodge's interiority makes for darkly comic and
scarifying radio drama and, although his monologues reveal him
to be monstrous (in one of the most arresting opening speeches on
radio he blithely uses the metaphor of serial-killing for surgery),
his exteriority presents a man of rote professionalism. Churchill
has referred to this strategy as a juxtaposition of subjects presented in and out of context, and in unstable and inconsistent
stage worlds that unexpectedly alter focus and shift between
naturalism and fantasy, and 'in and out of the more or less real'
(Gooch 1973: 40–41). This shifting of perspectival frames is a
strategy she has made her own and has experimented with
throughout her career, and absurdists such as Eugène Ionesco,
James Saunders and N.F Simpson are discernable as influences in
the background. As Churchill has explained in relation to *Owners*,
her first professional stage play in 1972, this focus-pulling
is designed to make audiences challenge received narratives and
discourses, and to reconsider their response to them. It is a form
of making the familiar strange but greatly extends Brecht's theory
of *Verfremdungseffekt* and is related to Diamond's notion of
'permissible visibility' discussed in Chapter 1.

> One of the things that happens is the juxtaposing of things that
> one accepts the existence of perfectly well if they're in their
> own context, set up against each other, they make each other
> absurd or unpleasant. And this in itself throws up a style which
> isn't naturalistic.[...] I think if people were more aware of the
> absurdities of positions they take as being quite normal,
> because it's what they do or because it's set up as a job – like
> dropping bombs because what you do in planes is drop
> bombs – if people were more aware of these things out of the
> context which makes them seem all right, then perhaps they
> wouldn't do them. An awful lot of horrible things people do
> are made to seem perfectly all right by their context, and that
> obviously makes them easier. If you could take the context
> away, it might make them harder.
>
> (Gooch 1973: 41)

Stripped of authority and sense, Hodge's work is exposed as straightforwardly destructive. In his last interior monologue and the end of the play, he plans to treat himself with aversion therapy in an attempt to kill an infatuation with Ellen (although he has previously confessed to 'well suppressed homosexual tendencies'), reveals that he is driven more by superstition than by science, and plainly intends to self-medicate to stave off suicide (*Shorts* 1990: 19). Hodge is a monstrous revenge-construct against the patriarchal 'authority' of conventional Freudian psychiatry.

By contrast, Weber, the psychiatrist in *Schreber's Nervous Illness*, shows restraint, intelligence and compassion for his patient Schreber, a distinguished doctor of law and a judge. Based on the *Memoirs of my Nervous Illness* by Daniel Paul Schreber written in 1903 (made famous by Freud's case history of 1911), Churchill's play offers a series of intense poetic insights into the judge's experience of schizophrenia. Schreber forensically examines his own thought processes and behaviours, and presents his insanity in a language of scientific rationalism while remaining quite unaware that what he is saying is clinically 'mad'. His descriptions of his dreads, phobias, experiences of possession, involuntary shouting and fitting, and his belief that he is slowly transforming into a woman, have their own patterns of narrative logic but reveal catastrophic dysfunctionality and disconnection. Radio is especially suited to the representation of interior worlds and Churchill's fascination with mindscapes and with the collision between cognitive perception and external realities was clearly stimulated in powerful ways at this time. The dramatisations of Schreber's delusional state are particularly evocative:

> My increasing nervousness attracted more and more souls, who lived in my head for a short time as little men and then dissolved in my body.
> RAY. I come from Cassiopeia
> RAY. From Gemma.
> RAY. From the Firmament.
> [...]
> And they dripped from the sky onto my head as thousands of little men.
>
> (*Shorts* 1990: 66)

Five other early radio plays *Identical Twins* (1968), *Abortive* (1971), *Not Not Not Not Not Enough Oxygen* (1971), *Henry's Past* (1972) and *Perfect Happiness* (1973) explore the relation between material calamity and interior worlds of denial and retreat. In *Identical Twins*, Churchill exploited recent developments in stereo sound and began initiating experiments in overlapping dialogue (for which she later became well known) to investigate the mental fragility of twins (played by the same actor, Kenneth Haigh) who feel that separate, autonomous identities are impossible. One is driven to suicide, the other is left, in many respects, leading the life of his dead twin. The play foreshadows *A Number* (2002), with its implicit philosophical meditation on self and otherness, and its performance challenges. Tydeman, the director, noted that Churchill's experimentalism in *Identical Twins* pushed the BBC in technically new ways: 'It required two overlapping monologues to be played by the same actor. It was complicated technically and something we hadn't tried before.'[4] *Abortive* has in its hinterland the controversies surrounding the legalisation of abortion and the nascent debates about male violence against women and the trauma of rape victims. The drama has echoes of Pinter's radio play *A Slight Ache* (1959), in which Flora's flirtation with a silent stranger might bring liberation or doom. In *Abortive*, the stranger, Billy, has stayed in the house at the husband's invitation, both husband and wife have developed an increasing fixation on him, and the wife, Roz, has been raped by Billy and undergone an abortion. Roz and Colin's relationship has broken down, although both are in denial, and the trauma of the rape and the termination gradually cost Roz her sanity. The play begins three weeks after the abortion, with Roz rejecting her husband's sexual advances, a moment the listener later understands to be emblematic of the psychological gulf between husband and wife. Roz, in fact, is manifesting all the signs of a depressive breakdown, suffering uncontrollable weeping, sleeplessness and feelings of guilt and horror. The rape is not describable, and the abortion not knowable: both have merged into the same unbearable pain. She knows that 'ghastly things' have been medically performed on her but cannot connect with reality: 'You miss all the unpleasantness. Like being dead' (*Shorts* 1990: 34). In her last monologue, symbolically delivered next to her sleeping husband, she reveals that she dreams of dying or being dead, that her life 'is a nightmare but with no content' and that she cannot rid herself of the anxiety that 'something's about to happen' (*Shorts* 1990: 36). In truth, something 'ghastly' has happened, both to her and to her relationship with her husband, and she may never recover.

Another character who endures a living death is Henry in *Henry's Past*. Burdened with a violent crime and a prison sentence in his past, Henry confesses that: 'I am in effect already dead, and the time to be lived until I die is only a fiction' (Roberts 2008: 40). The notion of the false self (an idea derived from Donald Winnicott and Laing), particularly socially constructed and imposed selves, as well as duplicitous selves created in matrimonial or other family settings, repeatedly appears in Churchill's work. In *Perfect Happiness* the ironically named Felicity is gradually revealed to be cowering behind an ideological construct of marriage as the apex of female self-fulfilment. Far from assertive and self-defining, Felicity is powerless, dependent and desperately vulnerable in the face of her husband's position of economic advantage. In *Not Not Not Not Not Enough Oxygen*, Mick and Vivian are literally dying from oxygen starvation in an apocalyptically polluted environment. Their lives have been reduced to a room in their tower-block flat, and when they watch Claude, Mick's son, commit a protest suicide, they can only reflect that his death 'might get a mention' on television (*Shorts* 1990: 55). The play is prescient of today's fixation with the suicide bomber, and the last focus on the television set foreshadows current obsessions with mediatised images and the spectacularisation of the real.

Experiments in television drama

Many are unaware that Churchill has written for television but between 1972 and 1981 she wrote six dramas: *The Judge's Wife* (1972), *Turkish Delight* (1974), *Save It for the Minister* (co-written with Cherry Potter and Mary O'Malley, 1975), *The After-Dinner Joke* (1978), *The Legion Hall Bombing* (1979) and *Crimes* (1982). Churchill appears to have found the producing structures in television oppressive and subject to a censorship that theatre and radio could negotiate with greater ease. She has also said that she has always been more excited by the liveness and physicality of theatre: 'I do like things that actually happen' (Kritzer 1991: 45). Always seeking to engage with formal and technical experiments, Churchill stretched her own skills by exploring flashback, flash forward, other visual and aural disjunctures, and documentary and multiple camera viewpoints. Characteristically, her own viewing preferences were for the innovative: 'I admired two extremes on TV, extreme naturalism and extreme non-naturalism – (Loach, Joffe; Monty Python)' (*Shorts* 1990: i). Churchill's themes were topical and hard-hitting, and she used the medium to interrogate legal systems and crime as a manifestation of political oppression, race and sex discrimination, marriage, the sex trade and women's disempowerment, capitalist excess, poverty, and charity organisations as profit-seeking multinationals (Kritzer 1991: 45–60).

Churchill's politics were painfully tested through the controversy surrounding *The Legion Hall Bombing*, a documentary play based on trial transcripts of a boy imprisoned for planting a bomb. The documentary exposed the cynical, stark prejudices of the so-called Diplock Courts in Northern Ireland introduced in 1973 to convict IRA and other 'terrorists' more easily. The boy was found guilty despite a witness who confirmed that he was 'definitely not' the boy whom he had witnessed placing the device, the police having apparently also falsified a confession (Kritzer 1991: 55). As Churchill has explained:

> The trial was extraordinary because there was no evidence to say the boy who was accused did it. There was no signed statement by him. There was no positive identification at all, and it was hard to believe you would get a conviction in a normal court. So I did a play for television with Roland Joffe; it meant reducing the nine and a half hours of trial transcript. We put on a voice-over at the beginning and end of the programme that explained the Diplock Courts, and the BBC took it off because they said it was political comment, and put up one of their own in different words, which they said was objective. We took our names off the credits as a protest.
>
> (Betsko and Koenig 1987: 81)

Churchill's voiceover set out the shady legality of the Diplock Courts in no uncertain terms: 'There is no jury. The judge sits alone. And the rules of evidence have been altered so that a confession is allowed as evidence even if it was obtained by threats or force' (Itzin 1980: 280). A blatant injustice had apparently been committed but the BBC, fearful of public protest and parliamentary censure, effectively gagged Churchill and Joffe, arguing that 'the play might aggravate tensions in Northern Ireland' (Itzin 1980: 280). The personal experience of that gagging resonates in her next television drama, *Crimes* – a bleak exploration of a futuristic world in which individual and collective protest are brutally suppressed and disabled. It is no surprise that Churchill continued to prefer the comparatively greater subversive potential and political freedoms of the stage.

Notes

1 Mark Lawson, *The Guardian*, 3 October 2012.
2 Mark Lawson, *The Guardian*, 3 October 2012.
3 The term 'anti-psychiatry' was coined not by Laing, as often reported, but by Laing's associate David Cooper – Laing never endorsed the term or Cooper's rejection of psychiatry *per se*. Alongside capitalist society (and all its applications in medicine, education, etc.), a major culprit in the etiology of madness as far as Laing is concerned, are the alienating and oppressive relationships found in some families, see also *Sanity, Madness and the Family* (London: Penguin, 1964) and *The Politics of Experience and the Bird of Paradise* (London: Penguin, 1967). Laing was himself greatly influenced by the work of Donald Winnicott, see *Family and Individual Development* (London: Tavistock, 1965).
4 Mark Lawson, *The Guardian*, 3 October 2012.

3 Stage Work in the 1970s

The end of empire and the post-war consensus

Like the 1960s, 1970s Britain was also characterised by the emergence of new self-confident and articulate socio-cultural configurations that manifested around issues of race, gender, sexuality, regional identity and ecology. One of the most notable configurations was the Women's Liberation Movement, which had a profound impact on Churchill. The International Women's Day marches in 1971 represented campaigns for equal pay, equal job and educational opportunities, free contraception and abortion on demand. Protest marches by numerous lobby groups were a feature of the decade and new legislation was subsequently introduced, including the Sex Discrimination Act (1975) and the Domestic Violence Act (1976). Racial discrimination, divisions and racially motivated attacks were frequently in the headlines and were inadequately dealt with by the Race Relations Act (1976). The new subcultures campaigned for radical change and accelerated the breakdown of the post-war consensus that had underpinned and ossified British society.

In *The Break-Up of Britain: Crisis and Neo-Nationalism* (1977), Tom Nairn famously argued that 1970s tendencies to political and social polarisation were a result of the protracted withdrawal from empire, and a failure to invest in and modernise trade, industry and public service institutions. The characteristics of the decade, Nairn asserted, were 'backwardness, economic stagnation, social decay, and cultural despair', and the rise of nationalism in Scotland and Wales were the direct consequences of post-imperial decline (Nairn

1977: 51). Internationally, the Cold War continued but with increased edginess following American defeat in Vietnam and expansion by the Soviet Union. Europe faced the phenomenon of urban terrorism in the form of the Red Brigades in Italy and Baader-Meinhof in Germany, as well as demands for political separatism from organisations such as the IRA in Ireland and ETA in the Basque country. The British government sought to counter international condemnation for the occupation of Northern Ireland by British troops in 1969, and stepped up their paramilitary operations as a result of IRA bombings, ambushes and other attacks.

In 1970 the newly elected Tory Prime Minister, Edward Heath, had promised a new style of government that would maintain the post-1945 consensual commitment to a mixed economy, full employment and the welfare state. The irony was that his progressiveness in securing Britain's entry to the European Union in 1973 also brought about his abandonment of lower taxes, lower spending and less intervention. The British economy struggled, suffering the worst stock market slump since the Second World War in 1973, serious surges in unemployment, and a damaging sterling crisis in 1976. Strikes began and ended the decade: the miners' strikes ending Heath's premiership in 1974, and the so-called 'winter of discontent' in 1978–79 forced out Labour prime minister Jim Callaghan – and indeed, the Labour Party, for a long time to come.

Churchill's trajectory as a playwright through the 1970s is framed through her leftist political resistance, a feature of which is her joyous discovery of collaborative theatre-making. While her plays resonate with protest and calls to individual accountability, Churchill also highlights the complexity of effecting change and the sacrifices required to act with political integrity.

Psychopathologies of colonisation: *The Hospital at the Time of the Revolution*

Hospital was written in 1972 but it took four decades for it to be premièred by director James Russell, at the Finborough Theatre, London, in 2013. The fiftieth anniversary of the end of the Algerian War in 2012 marked a new era of openness and on 19 March 2013 the French celebrated the first annual commemoration for all victims of the Algerian War. *Hospital* is a masterful study of the difficulty of political resistance in an oppressive imperial regime. The first of Churchill's plays to scrutinise revolutionary conditions and the psychological and physical abuse associated with authoritarian political systems, it manifests preoccupations to which she has repeatedly returned – the human rights of torture victims, and of those oppressed by domestic or international conflict, especially children (often female). *Hospital* is a sophisticated examination of the politics of complicity (an obsession with Churchill) and it is important to note the immediate tension between the utopian theorisation in her manifesto 'Not Ordinary, Not Safe', and her resistance to deploying heroising narratives in practice.

Hospital draws on the writings of the celebrated psychiatrist and champion of the Algerian struggle for independence, Frantz Fanon, who was not just an inspirational figure for black revolutionaries but also for Churchill's generation of white, Western political radicals in the 1960s (Macey 2007). The decolonisation of Africa had followed Indian independence in 1947, and the successful battle by the Algerian National Liberation Front (FLN) in 1954–62 to overthrow French imperialism and draw world attention to the plight of the victims (Connelly 2008). Churchill, born in 1938, grew up in this new, post-imperial world and was greatly influenced by Marxist revolutionary philosophies. Fanon himself did not live to see Algeria's liberation, but Churchill was 24 at the time, and it represented for her, as it did for many others, a historic moment of utopian possibility.

Set in the Blida-Joinville Hospital in Algeria, where Fanon was director of psychiatry from 1953 to 1956, *Hospital* offers an evocative representation of Fanon at work during the early phases of the revolution (Macey 2007). Visually, Churchill's description of the set – 'no scenery except bare white walls', 'white upright chairs', 'white beds for patients', 'bright light' – suggests that Churchill was well-acquainted with Fanon's *Dark Skins, White Masks* and his critique of the French policy of 'assimilation': Fanon's dark skin and the dark skins of his Algerian patients appear vulnerable in a symbolically imprisoning white glare (*Shorts* 1990: 97). Fanon is director of the facility but also its prisoner and warder, and the ironies inherent in his position become more complex as the play progresses. The difference between victim and perpetrator is not as straightforward as might first appear; even Fanon's mysterious silences, which at first seem to signal resistance, gradually begin to reveal a form of unavoidable complicity.

The characters whom Churchill's Fanon encounters have their origins in Alleg's famous account of the war available in the late 1950s (Alleg 2006); Fanon's *Black Skins, White Masks*; and case histories written by Fanon in his celebrated work on the Algerian revolution, *The Wretched of the Earth*, which was published in 1961 and rapidly came to serve as a model for other liberation struggles. In a remarkable chapter entitled 'Colonial War and Mental Disorders' Fanon anatomises the psychiatric disorders manifested by the so-called 'pacifiers' and the 'pacified' (Alexander et al 2002) and notes that there are significant similarities (Fanon 1967: 200–50). In fact, Fanon argues, the colonial project is itself a psychiatric phenomenon that proliferates mental illness, and necessitates abundant supplies of psychiatric specialists and hospitals. The colonial 'cure' of 'civilisation' is nothing other than 'a systematic negation of the other person', and apparent missionary philanthropy, in fact, conceals ruthless commercial exploitation (especially of oil) and mass de-humanisation (Fanon 1967: 200; Stora 2005; Horne 2006; Shepard 2008).

Churchill's construction of Fanon as a man of strategic reserve creates a stage presence that serves as a device to expose the pathologies of both the colonisers and the colonised: Europeans and Algerians talk to Fanon, their confessions revealing profoundly damaged psyches and a sense of self determined only by the ideology and practice of imperial aggression. Churchill's Fanon, like the actual man, cannot risk open resistance while at work without endangering his life. The hospital is a glass house of resonating tensions, a temporary refuge for the opponents and engineers of the regime, and it functions in a precarious state of limbo: Europeans and Algerians mix uneasily, always fearful of one another. By setting the play in the hospital, Churchill highlights the paradoxical and destructive circularity of a colonial system that asserts civilisation but is founded on pathological racism, insane loops of 'logic', and brutal oppression. Accordingly, Churchill's hospital becomes a metaphor for the self-devouring machine of imperialism, a microcosm of the much larger madhouse Algeria became under French rule.[1]

The Algerian patients Fanon treats in the play are symbolically without name or title and appear only as A, B and C. A is a resistance fighter, driven to bomb because he can see no other way to combat the enforced removal of his individual rights. Life in the FLN has separated him from his wife, family, job and home. He is wracked by the unbearable burden of having killed but para-doxically his sense of 'justice' compels him to continue killing. Trapped in this grotesque torment, he has tried but failed to end his own life. B has suffered a complete emotional and physical break-down from torture and is in clinical shock. He is terrified of further attack and cannot interact with others. He utters only a few lines and when he bumps into his ex-torturer, also receiving treatment at the hospital, he has to be prevented from committing suicide: 'Let me die. I can't go back there' (*Shorts* 1990: 146). C is constantly mistaken for a European because of his pale skin, experiences extreme guilt that he has not joined the resistance, and suffers paranoid delusions that other Algerians judge him to be both a coward and a traitor.[2] C's implosion is perhaps most drastic because he cannot connect with external reality at all, and his feel-ings of persecution are driven by profound self-loathing: 'What am I meant to do with my skin?' he asks despairingly (*Shorts* 1990: 142). All three cases indicate the dispossession and disintegration of self, which Fanon's writings describe in detail. Mental health is driven to breaking point because of the colonial task to erase the Algerian: 'colonialism forces the people it dominates to ask themselves the question constantly: "In reality, who am I?"' (Fanon 1967: 200). Once 'the point of no return' for an oppressed people is reached, argues Fanon in his essay, 'Concerning Violence', survival and self-definition can only be achieved through fighting back: 'The development of violence among the colonised people will be pro-portionate to the violence exercised by the threatened colonial regime' (Fanon 1967: 69).

The brutality of the Europeans whom Churchill's Fanon encounters is not in question: the Doctor, Police Inspector and the married couple Monsieur and Madame each demonstrate, in differ-ent ways, that torture and extermination are a norm and a patriotic duty. Monsieur was born in Algeria into a settler family but iden-tifies himself as French: 'This is my country. [...] I am already in France. France is Algeria' (*Shorts* 1990: 135). Monsieur is a civil servant and his settler status and occupation as one of the elite administrators of the colony almost certainly mean that he is also a substantial landowner.[3] He and his wife manifest a conditioned, ingrained racism, Monsieur viewing the colonial project as 'an endless struggle to curb and suppress and pacify' what he refers to as 'urban and rural elements', the children of whom are 'naturally born violent and dishonest' (*Shorts* 1990: 100–2):

> The violence is committed by criminals. It is not part of any revolution. The majority of the natives look to us to protect them and restore order. And it is only the French who can pacify the land. Because naturally the Algerian has criminal tendencies.
>
> (*Shorts* 1990: 110)

Defined entirely by racial prejudice and false doctrine, Monsieur and Madame cannot contemplate the success of the revolution, a concept outside their mental frame of reference, and yet the momentum of the liberation struggle places intolerable stress on their insistent patterns of denial. The breaking point threatens to be their daughter, Françoise, whom they bring to Fanon because she claims they are trying to kill her. Alleg has demonstrated that most sites of torture in the Algerian War were constructed within domestic settings (Alleg 2006). Slowly, the truth emerges and the spectator, cleverly positioned with an almost silent Fanon, comes to understand that the father is conducting interrogations, torture and executions in the family home: 'You won't find an area that has been so thoroughly cleared of subversive elements.' (*Shorts* 1990: 115). Françoise is kept awake by the torture sessions every night (the mother takes sleeping tablets). She abhors her parents' belief systems, and their denial of the fact that they are running a human slaughterhouse has triggered her schizophrenia.[4] As far as Monsieur and Madame are concerned, Françoise's trauma-induced insanity renders her a liability because it destroys her investment potential as 'a physically perfect specimen' whose unquestioning conformity will make her a natural inheritor of colonial Algeria (*Shorts* 1990: 100). Eventually Françoise's parents abandon her in the hospital, insisting that she cannot return home until she is engineered into the product they require. Françoise and Fanon are the only characters granted names in the play, and have a silent sympathy with one another: both are colonised in different fashions, but both are trying to resist oppression. For Churchill Françoise's fate looks bleak. A brilliantly haunting speech at the end of the play reveals her awareness that her own mother is symbolically murdering her by requiring her to wear the uniform of female conformity – by asking her to look pretty in her dress, play ignorant and stay quiet about the killing she knows her parents are perpetrating. Paradoxically, Francoise's speech signifies psychosis but, chillingly, the spectator knows that, even in her illness, she is saner than her psychopathic parents.

> The dress looked very pretty but underneath I was rotting away. Bit by bit I was disappearing. The dress is walking about with no one inside it. I undo the buttons and put my hand in. Under the dress I can't find where I am. So when I take it off there's nobody there. [...] My mother made that dress to kill me. It ate me away. That was a poison dress I put on.
>
> (*Shorts* 1990: 146)

In another dark twist, Fanon's two therapy sessions with the Police Inspector reveal a man who, like Monsieur, is defined by duty and profession. The revolution requires the Inspector's full-time expertise as a torturer. His transformation into a sadistic killing machine is evident from the lack of empathy he has for the Algerians he tortures or murders, as well as the pleasure he extracts from terrorising his wife and children. The Inspector's own diagnosis is tiredness caused by work stress, but the stress is connected in his mind with the need to demonstrate professional excellence, what he calls his 'flair': all he requires, he argues, are drugs to make him function efficiently and calmly (*Shorts* 1990: 143). The Inspector, then, will continue to work until his own catastrophic implosion, and Churchill's Fanon finds himself in the position of renewing a prescription designed to enable the Inspector to suppress all affect in order to kill more effectively. Fanon, in other words, has become the means by which the Inspector continues to function and is uncomfortably implicated in the oppression he seeks to resist. In *Toward the African Revolution* Fanon describes the colonial torturer's double-bind:

> Colonialism cannot be understood without the possibility of torturing, of violating or massacring. Torture is an expression and means of the occupant-occupied relationship [...]

> The police agent who tortures an Algerian infringes no law.
> His act fits into the framework of the colonialist institution. By
> torturing, he manifests an exemplary loyalty to the system.
>
> (Fanon 1964: 66, 71)

Fanon's own complicitous double-bind is revealed most by the
white, European Doctor, who cannot see the point in treating
'terrorists', and is deluded in his belief that by offering his medical
expertise to administer pentothal (the truth drug) to Algerians
under military interrogation, he will lessen their suffering and
curtail the war. He identifies wholly with the colonial regime, but
fails to conceive of himself as a soldier or torturer.[5] From Fanon's
perspective the Doctor is a war criminal who is steeped in the
unspeakable racial prejudice of Western medical science:

> The African is like a lobotomised European. It accounts for the
> impulsive aggression, the laziness, the shallowness of emotional
> affect, the inability to grasp the whole concept – the African
> character.
>
> (*Shorts* 1990: 119)

His self-deceiving speech justifying to himself the injection of pentothal as a licensed medical experiment, which will require him to
'observe the effects' in order to ascertain whether damage to
the personality can be limited (*Shorts* 1990: 132), is reminiscent of
the medical abuses under the Nazi and Soviet regimes. To the
Doctor, Algerian 'terrorists' are useful fodder for laboratory testing,
and Fanon's silences have exposed him as an enemy of the state –
the Doctor making it clear that Fanon's days are numbered: 'I'm
not threatening you [...] I just hope very much I never meet you as
one of the superintendent's patients' (*Shorts* 1990: 133).

Fanon's position as a psychiatrist was complicated by the fact
that he was a doctor of colour born in Martinique, but educated in
Paris. His education and accent gave him a status and authority not
accorded to other black doctors, but the institutional racism of
colonial medical practices coupled with systematic torture and
terror tactics by the authorities made it impossible for him to adopt
an effective mode of resistance while remaining in post. Churchill's
play ends with Fanon under threat. The real Fanon resigned and

joined the FLN, his letter of resignation providing a context for the
silences which are so poignant in the play:

> The events in Algeria are the logical consequence of an abortive
> attempt to decerebralise a people. [...] There comes a time when
> silence becomes dishonesty. [...] The decision I have reached is
> that I cannot continue to bear a responsibility at no matter what
> cost, on the false pretext that there is nothing else to be done.
>
> (Fanon 1964: 52–54)

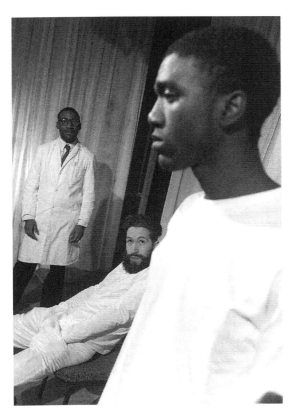

Figure 3.1 Miles Mitchell, Tim Pritchett and Benjamin Cawley in *Hospital
at the Time of the Revolution*, Finborough Theatre, London
© Alastair Muir

In her play, Churchill scrutinises both the futility of non-violent resistance and the disintegration of self that turning to violence can bring about. The real Fanon, a man who understood the relationship between personal accountability and political change, as well as the pain of accepting responsibility, displayed a complex self-knowledge and bold political conscience that Churchill evidently admired. Apparently, too politically incendiary for its time, it is interesting to reflect on why *Hospital* was finally considered safe enough for performance in 2013 – albeit at a fringe venue.

The fiftieth anniversary of the end of the Algerian War in 2012 gave rise to many events, special broadcasts and special publications in France and this is slowly having an effect across Western Europe. This is also a favourable era for celebrity and the obsession with the real, and the performing of real people by actors has become almost fetishised (Cantrell and Luckhurst 2010). However, it may be that Churchill's insistence on representing the colonised victim's dilemma of complicity, about which Fanon himself wrote at length, is still a challenge too far for mainstream theatre in times so bound by political correctness. Certainly, her refusal to erase questions of complicity in *Seven Jewish Children* as recently as 2009 became an international *cause célèbre*.

Owning up: capitalism and second wave feminism

Dispossession and ownership continued to be themes in Churchill's most well-known plays of the 1970s: *Owners*, *Light Shining in Buckinghamshire* and *Cloud Nine*.[6] Churchill has described the Royal Court theatre production of *Owners* in 1972 as 'a watershed': 'my working life feels divided quite sharply into before and after 1972' (*Plays 1* 1985: xi). Her first professional stage production, *Owners* also marked the beginning of a significant association with the Royal Court that has continued until this day. The production gave her visibility and led to her appointment as the first female Resident Dramatist at the Royal Court from 1974 to 1975 – a distinct achievement in such a consistently male-dominated organisation. It also brought together the personal and the political in new ways for Churchill: literally, in the sense that she wrote the play in three days still 'groggy' from the pain of a 'particularly gruesome late miscarriage' (Itzin 1980: 282); and theoretically in the sense that she explored current feminist thinking and, for a time, came to think of herself as a feminist writer (Aston 2001: 24). The late 1960s and early 1970s were years of extraordinary and intense political activity for second wave feminists and those changing contexts, themselves understood to be revolutionary, were of profound significance to Churchill.

In a foreword to *Owners* Churchill acknowledges her debt to Eva Figes, whose book, *Patriarchal Attitudes*, published in 1970, stands behind the construction of characters such as Marion, Clegg and Lisa (*Plays 1* 1985: 4). A classic text of the women's liberation politics of socialist second wave feminism, *Patriarchal Attitudes* appeared after Simone de Beauvoir's *The Second Sex*, Betty Friedan's *The Feminine Mystique* and Kate Millett's *Sexual Politics* but just before Germaine Greer's *The Female Eunuch*. Figes' book helped to break 'the taboo of silence' about women's subservience to men in Western, capitalist patriarchy (Figes 1970: 7). Figes' rage found an international audience: woman had been 'man-made', she argued:

> taught to desire not what her mother desired for herself, but what her father and all men find desirable in a woman. Not what she *is*, but should be. [...] The idea that a woman who does not find fulfilment in submitting herself utterly to the will of a husband and the demands of childbearing is somehow going against the natural order of things, is still with us.
>
> (Figes 1970: 17, 25).

Socialist second wave feminists made many of the same points as first wave feminists: the rise of capitalism was the root cause of modern social and economic discrimination against women; women were owned by their husbands; working-class women were the cheapest form of labour; marriage was a capitalist construction aimed at protecting male private property and lines of inheritance; and Freud had pathologised female sexuality and defined women as passive, reproductive machines. But second wave feminism also led to a widespread, organised network of politicised pressure groups, finding a groundswell of support at legislative level – times and public opinion had radically changed. Legates, for example, has argued that more social and political changes for women were accomplished in the 1960s and 1970s than in the previous two centuries (Legates 2001: 364).

Equally important to the background of *Owners* are the rental scandals of the 1950s and 1960s, about which the press ran stories of tenants who were paying extortionate rates for squalid housing and suffering harassment and eviction by ruthless landlords. Landlord Peter Rachman won notoriety for his intimidation tactics towards his tenants and the term 'Rachmanism' became a 1960s' watchword. In 1965 the Rent Act was introduced to mitigate the worst of the exploitation but problems persisted into the 1970s. When Churchill witnessed a blackmail attempt on an old woman offered money to vacate her rooms, she hatched both the play and the character of Worsely (*Plays 1* 1985: 4).

In *Owners*, husband and wife Marion and Clegg are defined by their blackly comic, rapacious desire to own property, business empires, other peoples' homes, minds, bodies and children. The influence of the cartoon worlds of grotesquery that Churchill imbibed from her father's profession are certainly evident in both characters. Described by Thomsen as a 'tragic farce' (Thomsen 1981: 166), the play shows an Ortonesque anarchy in both plot and dialogue as Marion and Clegg continually seek self-gratification through ruthless material and emotional exploitation of Lisa and Alec – 'love' is understood to be used and everyone is expendable. Marion is represented as a monstrous capitalist patriarch [sic], driven by an insatiable hunger for acquiring property; Clegg, appropriately a butcher by trade, is a sexual coloniser intent on using Lisa and delusional in his belief that he has a right to absolute ownership of his wife:

> She's not like other women in just one important respect. She's mine. I have invested heavily in Marion and don't intend to lose any part of my profit. She is my flesh.
>
> (*Plays 1* 1985: 56)

Marion and Clegg are different sorts of consumers from those represented in *Hospital*, and the issues of property ownership and tenancy have a 1970s British overlay, but their desires are familiar – the colonisation of bodies and land. In the light of the property booms in the 1990s and early 2000s, the ever-increasing divide between rich and poor, and evidence from the 2011 census that the English dream of home ownership is in decided retreat, Marion now makes a particularly disturbing theatrical impact.[7]

Collaboration with Joint Stock: *Light Shining in Buckinghamshire*

While *Hospital* focuses on the pathological difficulty of self-definition during the Algerian revolutionary struggle, *Light Shining in Buckinghamshire* explores the explosive potentialities for self-invention during the years of the English Civil War from 1642 onwards and the period of the English Republic from 1649 to 1660. *Light Shining* premiered in September 1976 at the Traverse Theatre in Edinburgh and is ambitiously experimental, the product of a famous collaboration with actors from Joint Stock. In it Churchill continues the search for forms that can best represent revolutionary outbreaks. As has been said, violent protest and mass demonstration as modes of expressing opposition to government regimes were features of the decade and need to be understood as the contemporary backdrop to the subject matter of the play (Megson 2012).

Set up by Max Stafford-Clark, David Aukin and David Hare, Joint Stock was the product of the proliferating phenomenon of alternative theatre, which had developed out of 1960s politicised countercultures. The proponents of alternative theatre companies had a specific interest in new, topical plays or performance events, and often sought out fresh constituencies through their touring strategies: playwrights such as David Hare, Howard Brenton, Bryony Lavery, John McGrath, Trevor Griffiths and David Edgar were all equally architects and participants (see Itzin 1980; Rees 1992; Trussler 1981; Kershaw 2004). Alternative theatre companies defined themselves against a mainstream conservatism, were bolder and more experimental in their stagings, and brought a variety to repertoire that changed the cultural landscape of British play selection. Joint Stock's methods of working, like John McGrath's company methods for 7:84, have been very influential on developing notions of political theatre in Britain. Their methods owed much to Erwin Piscator's and Brecht's collaborative models for enabling dramatists to produce more creative and politically charged plays

(Luckhurst 2006a: 109–51). Ritchie describes specific company methods in detail in *The Joint Stock Book*: the core ethos was developed by Bill Gaskill (who had been artistic director of the Royal Court) and Max Stafford-Clark, who insisted on methods of creating a play that incorporated the writer into a sustained workshop process with the actors for the purposes of enabling research and discussion about the generation of ideas and characters. The writer was not separated from the rehearsal process, as had often been the custom, and was understood as the figure at the centre of theatre-making. The intention was not just to produce a play but also to politicise collaborators and audiences through the process of production (Doty and Harbin 1990: 107–8).

Churchill's decision to work with Joint Stock stemmed from a political craving to find more committed creative environments, and the appeal of their touring policy with its outreach ethos (Doty and Harbin 1990: 155). She has recorded her 'intense pleasure' and 'excitement of being so crammed with ideas' in an account of the workshop process for *Light Shining*: 'I'd never seen an exercise or improvisation before and was as thrilled as a child at a pantomime' (Ritchie 1987: 118–21). She has also talked of the intensity of discussion and research:

> We had debates in the workshops and talks about specific historical characters. We read a lot and talked about moments of amazing change and extraordinariness in our own lives, things turned upside down. We got ourselves fluent with the Bible, so the whole area was opened up and everyone knew what it was about.
>
> (Itzin 1980: 282)

Churchill's production notes highlight the creativity of the actors and the strength of her partnership with director Max Stafford-Clark in the generation of ideas:

> The play is not improvised: it is a written text and the actors did not make up its lines. But many of the characters and scenes were based on ideas that came from improvisations at the workshop and during rehearsal. I could give endless examples of how something said or done by one of the actors is

directly connected to something in the text. Just as important, though harder to define, was the effect on the writing of the way the actors worked, their accuracy and commitment. I worked very closely with Max, and though I wrote the text the play is something we both imagined.

(*Plays 1* 1985: 184)

The experience of working so closely with the director and actors, and of making research visits to other communities and individuals, released her from feeling 'very solitary' as a writer (Betsko and Koenig 1987: 79) and was creatively life-changing:

I think it helped me in a direction that I wanted to go but found difficult, which was into more public areas of work. [...] If you're working by yourself, then you're not accountable to anyone but yourself while you're doing it. You don't get forced in quite the same way into seeing how your own inner feelings connect up with larger things that happen to other people. It was a mixture, I think, of the pressure to do that, and, with Joint Stock, researching something that threw up so much detail about a subject that I wouldn't myself have had the experience of, or perhaps even the confidence or even the curiosity to pursue in that kind of detail. [...] The work process is a double thing really: it has to do with your own inner obsessions, experiences, interests and the more public material which you can then explore.

(Cousin 1988: 4–5)

This period was vital in Churchill's discovery of the stimulus and inventiveness that actors could bring to her research and writing process; working collaboratively challenged her to cross into new creative territories.

Light Shining: history, revolution and the epic form

Given her political leanings, it was natural for Churchill to be drawn towards writing about a time of revolutionary fervour in her own country. *Light Shining* is the most straightforwardly Brechtian of all her plays in structure and acting concept. The main stage furniture consisted of six chairs and actors remained on stage throughout, observing the action and effecting costume changes in full view of the audience. Churchill and Stafford-Clark might be said not to have heeded Brecht's warnings that plays should not carry their research too heavily. The play assumes an informed knowledge of ideas prevalent in the Civil War and is unashamedly demanding. This does not make it any the less fascinating or dramatically effective and its premiere run was extended, but Stafford-Clark felt that while the production had a look of beautiful Brechtian austerity it lacked Brecht's clarity and precision of narrative, and might even be 'boring' (Roberts and Stafford-Clark 2007: 27). At the New York Theater Workshop premiere of *Light Shining* in 1991 the American critic Mel Gussow reflected that the challenges inherent in both form and content made it a dense and disorienting play that is 'interesting' but received with difficulty by other cultures.[8] Perhaps compensating for overburdened content, the New York Theater Workshop focused on creating a Brechtian aesthetic – a strikingly sparse design with a 'Shaker-like simplicity: a table that when upended serves as a pulpit; chairs that are hung on pegs [...] and bells are rung as a call to arms and meetings.'[9] Although the play presents tough production challenges, this has only made it even more of a tantalising puzzle to many directors and theatre companies.

In *Light Shining*, the carefully patterned narrative threads of *Hospital* are replaced by flashes of character, glimpses into interior worlds and snatches of varying external realities. The play presents a kaleidoscopic set of perspectives and includes documentary inserts and direct quotation from seventeenth-century pamphlets, which are juxtaposed with vignettes of everyday encounters and political and religious debates extraordinary for their frankness. Actors play multiple roles; some characters are recreations of historical figures and some are inventions. Churchill's stage notes explain the notion of a montage effect, but her structure differs from a theory of Brechtian montage, which posits scenes as separate units but within a more tightly knit grander narrative in which, even with multiple role-play, the same characters are normally played by the same actor. Churchill's perspectival model builds in a structural multi-focality that is highly unusual and explores a form that is both suited to the subject matter of turbulence and reflexively shows its own fractures to a much greater extent.

The characters are not played by the same actors each time they appear. The audience should not have to worry which actor they are seeing. Each scene can be taken as a separate event rather than part of a story. This seems to reflect better the reality of large events like war and revolution where many people share the same kind of experience.

(Plays 1 1985: 184–85)

For the historian Christopher Hill, the 1640s and early 1650s represent 'the greatest upheaval that has yet occurred in Britain' and saw 'a great overturning, questioning, revaluing of everything in England' (Hill 1991:13–14). Churchill concentrates on the revolution that did not happen – what Hill terms 'the revolt within the Revolution' (Hill 1991: 15). She explains the trajectory of the play in her foreword:

For a short time when the king had been defeated anything seemed possible, and the play shows the amazed excitement of people taking hold of their own lives, and their gradual betrayal as those who led them realised that freedom could not be had without property being destroyed.

(Plays 1 1985: 183)

The reflexive, interrogatory structure of *Light Shining* asks its spectators to draw parallels with their own lives and times. Had the revolt within the Revolution succeeded, it would have radically changed England's political course, perhaps ultimately legalising communal property, disestablishing the Church and disavowing the Protestant ethic, as well as instituting a far more extensive legal and political democracy. By contrast, the Revolution that took root established the sacred rights of property (with the abolition of feudal tenures), gave political power to the propertied (through sovereignty of Parliament and common law), and 'removed all impediments to the triumph of the ideology of the men of property – the protestant ethic' (Hill 1991: 15). These changes ensured a new focus on capital and prepared the way for England to become the first industrialised great power.[10] Churchill, a playwright living in the aftermath of empire and critical of the course taken, imagines a great historical 'what if'.

Churchill's attention is on the religious radicals, and on power-fully renewed millenarian beliefs exacerbated initially by Charles I's defeat and then his execution in 1649. The millennium, believed to be imminent, meant the fall of the Antichrist, the second coming, and a period of heaven on earth when Jesus would reign for a thousand years.[11] These views might appear strange to us but reli-gious conflicts seem no less imminent in the twenty-first century, and the divide between fundamentalism and atheism no less extreme. *Light Shining* provides evocative glimpses of the anti-clerical worlds of such sectaries as the Levellers, Diggers and Ran-ters, the radical elements in Oliver Cromwell's New Model Army, the laity, the vagrant and the poor, as well as portraying Cromwell and his commissary general, Ireton.

It is not difficult to see why the intellectual and moral revolution begun in the years of Civil War, and incited further by millenar-ianism, came to be regarded as seditious by the politicised, land-owning hierarchy. The main subjects of debate were religion, liberty and property – all three were inextricably linked and the efforts of agitators such as the Levellers centred on examining the preconceptions behind their inter-relationship. Morton describes the Levellers as 'the first fully democratic party in the Revolution', whose insistence on 'freedom of the pulpit' ensured the dis-semination of democratic and revolutionary ideas (Morton 1970: 12).[12] Leveller influence was powerful in the socially mobile Model Army and helped to turn it into a 'short-lived school of political democracy' (Hill 1991: 128), where social injustices were hotly debated and significant numbers of soldiers became political edu-cators and preachers, speaking to peasants of civil liberties, reli-gious toleration, election issues and of the wrongs of private land enclosure and disafforestation that had penalised the poor and starving (Brailsford 1961). All these issues continue to resonate in democratic and non-democratic countries today, and depending on circumstances, the modern equivalents of the Levellers might be branded terrorists.

The play crackles with the energy of numerous characters exchanging incendiary ideas and embarking on journeys of unpre-cedented self-discovery. Hoskins, for example, argues with a preacher that Calvinist notions of predestination are unfounded and unfair, and suggests that sickness and death have a great deal more to do with mismanagement by those in power than with sin and divine purpose: 'How can God choose us from all eternity to be saved or damned when there's nothing we've done?' (*Plays 1* 1985: 202, 205). Claxton, based on the real-life Laurence Clarkson, known as 'Captain of the Rant', explains that god is 'an infinite nothing', and that 'sin' has to be committed to demonstrate that it is non-existent: 'I have come to see that there is no sin but what man thinks is sin.' (*Plays 1* 1985: 207). Two women, inside the house of a rich landowner who has fled, talk of burning the legal papers that detail how the property was consigned to him: 'That's like him burnt. There's no one over us' (*Plays 1* 1985: 207). The scene establishes a fundamental link between identity and property. The women's realisation that they and other commoners are standing on the brink of an extraordinary revolutionary moment is symbolised by their discovery of a large mirror. Neither woman has ever seen herself before because mirrors are luxury items, and Churchill uses the image to convey them in a moment of transformative personal and political self-knowledge. This is a moment which brilliantly illuminates Brecht's notion of Gestus – it refracts a material, economic history as well as a legal narrative of women's historic struggle to define themselves as equal to men. 'You see your whole body at once. You see yourself standing in that room. They must know what they look like all the time. And now we do.' (*Plays 1* 1985: 207)

The war of ideas is played out in the remarkable scene that completes Act I, which represents an edited snapshot of the so-called Putney debates, when members of the Model Army assembled at a church in Putney, London, on 28 October 1647. At this time the Army included delegates at both senior and junior officer level elected by the rank and file, and Leveller ideas were at their most pervasive. The issue of central importance was the question of franchise, namely, the question of exactly who was entitled to elect the sovereign parliament. Churchill represents just six of the original participants: Levellers Colonel Rainborough, Edward Sexby, John Wildman, and Cromwell, General Ireton and Colonel Rich. Rainborough argues that the poor and unpropertied live in a state of complete subjection, as do soldiers who have fought for parliament against the monarchy but are disbarred from any process of direct election:

all Englishmen must be subject to English law, and the foundation of the law lies in the people [...] The old law of England [...] enslaves the people of England – that they should be bound by laws in which they have no voice! And for my part, I look upon the people of England so, that wherein they have not voices in the choosing of their governors they are not bound to obey them.

(Plays 1 1985: 213–14)

Sexby, a private, is even more critical, voicing the betrayal felt by thousands of soldiers who have not fought primarily to protect property but for their status as citizens:

It seems now except a man hath a fixed estate in the kingdom, he hath no right in this kingdom. [...] If we had not a right to the kingdom, we were mercenary soldiers. [...] If this thing be denied the poor, that with so much pressing after they have sought, it will be the greatest scandal. It was said that if those in low condition were given their birthright it would mean the destruction of this kingdom. I think the poor and meaner of this kingdom have been the means of preservation of this kingdom.

(Plays 1 1985: 215–16)

But it is Ireton who wins the day, covertly supported by Cromwell, who postulates that property is neither bestowed by the law of God, nor by the law of nature but 'is of human constitution': 'I have a property and this I shall enjoy' *(Plays 1* 1985: 215). Ownership of land, for Ireton, invests its proprietor with a right to govern, and, in turn, commoners have a right to be governed by those 'that have the interest in the kingdom' *(Plays 1* 1985: 216–17). The meeting is a defeat for the Levellers, and Rainborough sums up his despair with a poignant observation: 'I see it is impossible to have liberty without all property being taken away' *(Plays 1* 1985: 216). In this moment of history, possession of private property is enshrined as the principle that guarantees a man or woman's legal enfranchisement.

Act II opens with a narration of one of the most celebrated, radical stands against private property – the Diggers' protest at St George's Hill in Surrey in 1649, when Gerrard Winstanley spearheaded the digging and sowing of private land. In a speech that was predicated on republican beliefs and a proactive bid to address the needs of the poor, Winstanley argued that England could not be free until commoners had the licence to cultivate the land and feed themselves. Winstanley's model of a self-sufficient community living according to its own religious and political philosophies was an early example of communism: 'there can be no universal liberty till this universal community be established' (*Plays 1* 1985: 219). Significantly, the title of the play, *Light Shining in Buckinghamshire*, refers to a Leveller pamphlet calling for equality of property in 1648. Cromwell wasted no time in routing the Diggers and destroying both their houses and their cultivated land; Leveller resistance was finally crushed at Burford in the same year. After 1649 parliamentarians became more hard-line and radical elements in the Army and among the people were either marginalised or brutally stamped out. Act II reports the steady stream of defeats and the decline in radicalism and its material effects. A wide range of characters testify to the regression. Ideologically opposed to the war in Ireland, Briggs deserts the Army, his views now regarded as dangerously dissident. Brotherton, a vagrant, is still destitute and symbolically cannot shake herself free of the belief that she is damned for killing the baby she could not afford to nurture. Another woman cannot abandon her baby even though she knows it will die of starvation if she keeps it. The Ranters briefly find a form of utopianism in the sexual liberty that they espouse: 'we'll have no property in the flesh' (*Plays 1* 1985: 234) but are later pursued and persecuted. In an epilogue set after the restoration of the king in 1660, characters reveal their broken spirits in a moving lamentation. Briggs has become a fugitive and survives by eating grass. Brotherton is still forced into criminality to make a living. Claxton rues the curtailment of free speech, Hoskins wonders how they missed their opportunity for change, and Cobbe, the Ranter, reflects on the introduction of legislation to reinforce Protestantism (*Plays 1* 1985: 240–41). As Churchill says in her foreword, this is far from heaven on earth: 'what was established instead was an authoritarian parliament, the massacre of the Irish, the development of capitalism' (*Plays 1* 1985: 183). In her play, Churchill gives a set of vivid insights into the failed struggle for liberty.

Hill has given a trenchant summation of how different the world might have been if the Ranters had won:

> We can discern shadows of what this counter-culture might have been like. Rejecting private property for communism, religion for rationalistic and materialistic pantheism, the mechanical philosophy for dialectical science, asceticism for unashamed enjoyment of the good things of the flesh, it might have achieved unity through a federation of communities, each based on the fullest respect for the individual. Its ideal would have been economic self-sufficiency, not world trade or world domination.
>
> (Hill 1991: 341)

In *Light Shining*, Churchill examines a moment when the potential for political change was passionately believed in but thwarted, and the parallels with the protests and demonstrations of the 1960s and 1970s are clear. At the end of the play in the brief few speeches following the restoration of the monarchy entitled 'After', there is disillusionment and a return to the struggle simply to stay alive. Claxton has significantly lost his faith in words and utters the last line of the production: 'My great desire is to see and say nothing' (*Plays 1* 1985: 241). In a final dark note, Churchill seems to call herself to silence and reminds her spectators, as she has done through the very form of the play, that they are active witnesses, who are being called to question their own complicity with or contestation of politics in their own era.

Feminism, reproduction and the politics of medicine: Monstrous Regiment and *Vinegar Tom*

Churchill's decision to write a play set during seventeenth-century witch-hunts drew on material she was reading for *Light Shining*. Churchill began work with the collective feminist theatre group Monstrous Regiment, having met them after a pro-abortion march (Hanna 1991: xxxvii). Born out of the Women's Liberation Movement of the 1960s and 1970s, Monstrous Regiment was one of the most high-profile of numerous feminist theatre companies in Britain founded to combat political, institutional and social discrimination against women (Goodman 1993). The company sought not simply to raise consciousness about women's issues through their touring strategy but also to offer more opportunities for female writers, actors and directors and to change the material conditions of play selection and production. Significantly, the play premiered in the north and in the working-class city of Hull at the Humberside Theatre in 1976. The process was 'one of the happiest' Monstrous Regiment ever knew (Hanna 1991: xxxvii), and left Churchill 'stimulated by the discovery of shared ideas [...] and possibilities in the still new company' (*Plays 1* 1985: 129). As with Joint Stock, Churchill was enlightened by her creative journey with this feminist collective (which included men), who enabled her to orientate her writing more towards constructing exterior worlds for the stage (as opposed to the mindscapes she had been used to writing for radio). She has expressed her debt to Monstrous Regiment unequivocally: 'my attitude to myself, my work and others had been basically and permanently changed' (*Plays 1* 1985: 131). Churchill began to develop a greater emotional distance from her writing, and to sharpen her dramaturgical and critical skills in relation to her own work:

> Discussing with Monstrous Regiment helped me towards a more objective and analytical way of looking at things. Their attitude to the witches was in terms of economic pressure and the role of women in that society. They ensured that I approached the witchcraft in a cool analytical frame of mind. I was more aware than I had been before of what I was doing.
>
> (Itzin 1980: 285)

The socially and politically constructed idea of 'the witch' appealed to her because it fitted well with 1970s' feminist discourses that presented women as oppressed and scapegoated victims of patriarchal systems. In *Patriarchal Attitudes*, Figes argued:

> Woman as a source of danger, as a repository of externalised evil, is an image that runs through patriarchal history. She is witch, demoness, scarlet woman, schemer, and her power in the minds of men usually increases in inverse proportion to her actual power in the world of reality.
>
> (Figes 1970: 45)

Churchill was struck by 'the connections between medieval attitudes
to witches and continuing attitudes to women in general. The women
accused of witchcraft were often on the edges of society, old, poor,
single, sexually unconventional' (*Plays 1* 1985: 129–30). Those connections are brought to life by Churchill's dialectical structure, which
juxtaposes a stylised, antiquated dialogue delivered in historical costume with contemporary songs performed by the same actors in
modern dress. The songs, Churchill explains, 'are not part of the
action and not sung by the characters in the scene before them' (*Plays
1* 1985: 133). They vary in mood but explore the themes of the play:
the demonisation of female sexuality; the witch as the personification
of a discourse that positions women as evil; 'madness' as a manifestation of societal misogyny; the struggle for self-determination; and
medical intervention as a form of patriarchal control. For Churchill
Vinegar Tom is 'a play with no witches in it'; instead, she argues, it
is about 'poverty, humiliation and prejudice' (*Plays 1* 1985: 130).
Vinegar Tom brings past and present, as well as different linguistic
registers and performance styles into collision in order to convey that
as capitalism has progressed the ideological and material battles faced
by women are no different from those in eras perceived as 'unen-
lightened'. Written very much with female audience members in
mind, the songs directly invite political activism:

> Look in the mirror tonight.
> Would they have hanged you then?
> Ask how they're stopping you now.
> Where have the witches gone?
> Ask how they're stopping you now.
> Here we are.

> (*Plays 1* 1985: 176)

The construct of the witch also allowed Churchill to continue her
examination of state-sanctioned pathologies of demonisation and
'cure' as state instruments of control and terror. A 'strong influence'
was a polemical pamphlet written by Barbara Ehrenreich and
Deirdre English entitled *Witches, Midwives, and Nurses: A History
of Women Healers* (1973) (*Plays 1* 1985: 129). In this pamphlet,
Ehrenreich and English represent the vilification and mass murder
of supposed 'witches' from the fourteenth to the seventeenth

century as a systematic and brutal suppression of women designed to subjugate populaces. What was arresting about their argument was their insistence that witches were effectively medical practitioners (and often skilled midwives) for communities who had no doctors or hospitals (Ehrenreich and English 1973: 13). The female healer, they postulated, was seditious because of her empirical approach and her belief in trial and error, an ideological position contrary to the faith and obedience doctrines promulgated by Church and state. Ehrenreich and English linked witch-hunting with the 'devastating exclusion' of women from independent healing roles and the creation of a new male-dominated medical profession that has continued a practice of violent, medicalised pacification of women to the present day (Ehrenreich and English 1973: 6).

> the suppression of women health workers and the rise to dominance of male professionals … was an active takeover by male professionals … [13] The stakes of the struggle were high: political and economic monopolisation of medicine meant control over its institutional organisations, its theory and practice, its profits and prestige. And the stakes are even higher today, when total control of medicine means potential power to determine who will live and who will die, who is fertile and who is sterile, who is 'mad' and who is sane.
>
> (Ehrenreich and English 1973: 4)[14]

Churchill's own medical history of miscarriage had given her personal insights into the healthcare system and into the tendency to pathologise pregnancy as 'illness'. She was herself also negotiating the politics of domesticity at home. In *Vinegar Tom*, the only route to social acceptance for women of all classes is domestic and marital confinement within a misogynistic Christian tradition that insists on the inferiority of women to men. That inferiority is premised on the supposed biological perversity of the female body and its associated uncontrollably debased sexual appetites. The female is inherently 'sinful' because she is not male and her role in life is to accept punitive confinement – any woman seeking to identify herself outside these parameters is deemed insane or evil. Thus Marjory, a petty and superstitious peasant, subscribes wholly to propaganda and shops Joan to the witch-finder. Ellen, a lone elderly healer, and

Joan, desperately poor, dispossessed and reduced to begging for food, are both hanged. Susan is convinced that she is a witch because she has taken potions to induce an abortion, and believes that her salvation lies in execution. Betty, a landowner's daughter, is treated for hysteria and subjected to terrifying sessions of forced blood-letting because she is resisting marriage:

> Why am I tied? Tied to be bled. Why am I bled? Because I was screaming. Why was I screaming? Because I'm bad. Why was I bad? Because I was happy. Why was I happy? Because I ran out by myself and got away from them.
>
> (*Plays 1* 1985: 149)

Betty's daily 'treatment', which is a form of torture, coupled with her indoctrination into believing that she can be saved from her evil nature by subjugating herself to the prescribed passivity of the domestic sphere, ensure her survival. Only Alice, after Ellen's death, is defiant, realising that they are all the victims of a pathological desire to control and destroy any sign of female independence. Alice also recognises that she can only challenge the status quo by becoming the Other: 'I'm not a witch. But I wish I was [...] There's no way for us except by the devil.' (*Plays 1* 1985: 175). A powerful feminist piece, which sometimes suffers from some rather clichéd notions of how its characters might be represented,[15] *Vinegar Tom* again borrows from Brecht's theory of epic structure but goes beyond it through introducing colliding time zones and different performance styles.[16] The final scene is particularly biting in its political message; it is an uproarious music hall double-act in which women play the male authors of the infamous *Malleus Maleficarum*, the misogynistic tract that fuelled many killings.[17] The fact it is delivered by women sending up the men who would have undoubtedly put them to death in the past, is a carnivalesque celebration of the success of feminist movements, but also a reminder to female spectators that current freedoms should not be taken for granted.

SPRENGER:	He's Kramer.
KRAMER:	He's Sprenger.
KRAMER/SPRENGER:	professors of Theology
KRAMER:	delegated by letters apostolic

SPRENGER:	(here's a toast, non-alcoholic)
KRAMER:	Inquisitors of heretical pravities
SPRENGER:	we must fill those moral cavities
KRAMER:	so we've written a book
SPRENGER:	*Malleus Maleficarum*
KRAMER:	*The Hammer of Witches*
SPRENGER:	It works like a charm
KRAMER:	to discover witches
SPRENGER:	and torture with no hitches

(*Plays 1* 1985: 176)

Vinegar Tom is a standard text for many schools, universities and conservatoires. It prefigured Elaine Showalter's *The Female Malady* (1987) and Jane Ussher's *Women's Madness: Misogyny or Mental Illness?* (1991) in fascinating ways, and it foreshadowed debates about prejudices towards older women spurred by Germaine Greer's *The Change: Women, Ageing and the Menopause* (1991). *Vinegar Tom* also continues to feed into educational debates about women's rights to determine their own medical treatment, a particularly controversial issue in the realms of gynaecology and obstetrics. Greer's conviction that the cultural signifier of 'the old witch', although 'found in every human society,' is more deep-rooted in developing countries and 'peoples who have no explanation of infertility, sickness and death' than in the developed world, is strangely reductive (Greer 1991: 390). Interestingly, Western cultures are ever more fixated on generating artistic constructions of the witch, as *Wicked* and *Oz*, demonstrate. 'Why not befriend a toad today?' asks Greer (1991: 412). Churchill, I suspect, would advise something more radical, and her creation of Betty in *Cloud Nine* certainly continued her interest in drawing attention to the social erasure of older women.

Notes

1 Algeria was not considered a colony *per se* but a French province. Its political status, on the one hand, and the presence of an important minority of French settlers, on the other, made the war quite unlike any other anti-colonial war.
2 The FLN gave the most dangerous jobs to those with pale skin because it was harder for French paratroopers to detect them.

3 Fanon saw the civil service as a strategic means of implementing colonial oppression. Ironically, as director of Blida Hospital he was himself a civil servant.

4 Similarities between schizophrenic symptoms and trauma related to torture are well documented by clinicians treating torture victims.

5 See 'Medicine and Colonialism' in Fanon's *A Dying Colonialism* (New York: Grove Press, 1965).

6 *Owners* was followed by two plays that also explored attack and resistance. *Objections to Sex and Violence* (1975) was the first of Churchill's plays to be presented on the Royal Court's main stage, and investigated anarchism and violent protest; *Moving Clocks Go Slow* (1975) premiered on the Royal Court studio stage and focuses on an attack on Earth by aliens (Kritzer 1991: 67–76).

7 On the census results, see Philip Collins, 'Five Questions for Britain' in *Prospect*, February 2013: 26–29.

8 Mel Gussow, *New York Times*, 17 February 1991.

9 Mel Gussow, *New York Times*, 17 February 1991.

10 See also Christopher Hill, *God's Englishman: Oliver Cromwell and the English Revolution* (London: Weidenfeld and Nicholson, 1970) and *The Intellectual Origins of the English Revolution Revisited* (Oxford: Clarendon Press, 1997).

11 See Norman Cohn, *The Pursuit of the Millennium* (London: Temple Smith, 1970).

12 In the seventeenth century, the sermon was the most important means of spreading politico-religious ideology. Pamphlets and improvements in printing presses were also extremely important in the battle of ideas.

13 Women were disbarred from professionalisation when university training for medicine became mandatory.

14 This work has now been superseded by a rich seam of scholarship, see, for example, Patricia Crawford, *Women and Religion in England 1500–1720* (London: Routledge, 1993); Lyndal Roper, *Oedipus and the Devil* (London: Routledge, 1994); Margaret Sommerville, *Sex and Subjection* (London: Arnold, 1995); Natalie Davis, *Women on the Margins* (Cambridge: Harvard, 1995); Robin Briggs, *Witches and Neighbours* (London: HarperCollins, 1996).

15 Gillian Hanna of Monstrous Regiment has explained that the political messages were unapologetically heavy-handed because they did not want to 'allow the audience to get off the hook' in telling a history of male oppression (Aston 2001: 29).

16 For a study of Brechtian devices in *Vinegar Tom* see Reinelt (1996).

17 Churchill noted in a later interview that she had been surprised at the lack of available comic models for female double-acts, see *Time Out*, 29 October–3 November 1977.

4   Key Production: *Cloud Nine*

Cloud Nine followed *Traps* (1977) at the Royal Court Theatre Upstairs and contributions to Monstrous Regiment's feminist cabaret, *Floorshow* (1977). *Traps* sets up and then confounds realist conventions in narrative, structure, character and the materiality of the stage world. *Floorshow*, driven by a desire to explore women's comedy and to investigate whether 'there was such a thing as "women's theatre"' (Hanna 1991: xxxix) challenged the male-dominated territory of stand-up comedy. Both these projects proved fertile ground for rehearsing devices that Churchill used in *Cloud Nine*.

In *Cloud Nine* Churchill extends her experiments with time-frames, comedy and role play to explore the possibility of contemporary (1970s) sexual self-definition. Another collaboration with Max Stafford-Clark and Joint Stock, it was first performed at Dartington College of Arts in February 1979 and then toured. In his new position as artistic director of the Royal Court, Stafford-Clark revived the play for a London run in 1980: it initially bemused the critics but its striking form, character doublings and explicit, timely content struck a chord with audiences and it became an unexpected hit. In 1981 Tommy Tune directed the American premiere at Lucille Lortel's Theater de Lys in New York, where it ran for a year, attracting major awards including three OBIEs. In 1982 *Cloud Nine* played in New Zealand, Japan, Denmark, West Germany and Belgium. In 1983 it opened in Brazil. *Cloud Nine* brought Churchill international attention and it remains one of her most controversial works.

Workshop process

The idea to concentrate the preliminary three-week workshop process on sexual politics came from Churchill herself (Roberts and Stafford-Clark 2007: 68). Stafford-Clark initially thought it was a subject matter more suited to a feminist company or a female director; 'Joint Stock at that time was such a male company and no one seemed to think about issues of that kind at all', but he rapidly realised that his own assumptions begged inquiry.[1] In Stafford-Clark's account of the workshop, based on his diary entries, actors were selected 'as much for their sexual proclivities as for their acting ability' (Roberts and Stafford-Clark 2007: 69), workshop membership comprising a heterosexual married couple, a gay male couple, a lesbian, two bisexual men, two heterosexual women and a heterosexual man.[2] Stafford-Clark lists himself as a member of the group but interestingly not Churchill, although obviously she was present throughout and identified herself as a 'heterosexual feminist socialist' (Roberts and Stafford-Clark 2007: 70).

The relationship between the workshop exercises and the eventual play, written at home in the following 12 weeks, is very difficult to establish, and the subject of a degree of myth-making. In her foreword to *Cloud Nine*, Churchill is clear that the workshops concentrated on further research and exploration of sexual politics (subject matter about which she was already very well informed) and that the writing was a separate process (apart from rewrites during a subsequent six-week rehearsal period). The workshops involved sharing attitudes and experiences, exploring stereotypes and role reversals, and talking to individuals outside the group. Writing the play Churchill returned to a private obsession, 'the parallel between colonial and sexual oppression', and an interest in the French dramatist and man of letters Jean Genet (1910–86), who had described 'the colonial or feminine mentality of interiorised repression' – an idea that had been touched on only briefly during the workshop (*Plays 1* 1985: 245). The play's situations and characters, then, were not developed in the workshops, but Churchill acknowledges that the play 'drew deeply' from them (*Plays 1* 1985: 245). The title of the play came from a story told to workshop members by the female cleaner of the rehearsal space, who one day offered to tell her own story of a violent marriage and a subsequent relationship in which she achieved orgasm for the first time and felt on 'cloud nine'.[3] That story inspired the character of Betty, in many ways the least caricatured figure.

For the actors the subject of sexual politics, which Antony Sher interpreted from the workshop process to mean 'attitudes towards sex', proved to be a baptism of fire – especially since the group members were themselves the primary research material (Ritchie 1987: 141). Thus Miriam Margolyes recalled 'laughter and terror' and 'the "truth sessions" – sitting in a circle each day, one of us in the middle, telling everything about our lives, our sexuality, and our insecurities – trusting a group of near strangers with buried secrets and private fears' (Ritchie 1987: 138). In fact, a striking feature of most of the fragmented accounts by actors (which are rather problematically mediated by Ritchie and Stafford Clark[4]) is the terrifying intensity of what individuals revealed both about their sexual experiences and themselves and what was revealed to them by others. They have described the workshops as an emotional rollercoaster: 'rewarding but totally terrifying'; 'very very traumatic [...] very satisfying'; 'early on I was freaked' (Roberts and Stafford-Clark 2007: 86–87). Subjects discussed during those three weeks were the workshop members' own childhoods, their parents' attitudes to sex, their own sexual experiences and orientations, sexual partnerships and casual encounters, masculinity, the stress of child-rearing and parenting, and their fears or hostility towards the opposite sex (Roberts and Stafford-Clark 2007: 68–96). The power structure of actors improvising for the director was sometimes painfully apparent and certain actors felt vulnerable to criticism because the improvisation exercises could have extremely personal resonances. Margolyes found the time both bruising and productive: 'It was a spurious democracy – he [Stafford-Clark] had the real power but he did try to make us take the responsibility' (Ritchie 1987: 138). At the end of the process one of the workshop members said that they were 'surprised by the amount of trauma' it all entailed (Roberts and Stafford-Clark 2007: 86).

Over time those actors have become increasingly unwilling to talk about the process of making *Cloud Nine*. Only in the act of writing up the workshop 25 years later did Stafford-Clark realise that he had effectively written down 'the confidence of the confessional' and that publication of his diary notes might be akin to setting off a ticking bomb (Roberts and Stafford-Clark 2007: 69).[5] Unsure how to articulate the process but knowing it to be quite different from anything else he had ever undertaken, Stafford-Clark settled for the significant formulation that 'the territory of the workshop over-lapped with group therapy' and wrote that by the end 'we were emotionally drained' (Roberts and Stafford-Clark 2007: 96). The process of *Cloud Nine*, therefore, has become as famous for its 'traumatic' nature as for arguments about whether it was or wasn't politically enlightening for its workshop members. In its day Stafford-Clark's workshop had the dynamics of 1970s' collective discussion (with all the attendant political snares). Sher has given perhaps the most cogent account of how he saw the actors' journeys:

> Throughout the workshop we each took turns to tell our own life stories and to answer questions on our sexual experiences and lifestyles. It was nerve-wracking to contemplate (and far more revealing than stripping naked would have been) and so it is to the credit of the group that these sessions became the most exhilarating of all. Through each of them the real meaning of sexual politics was becoming clear. Each of us was secure in our own separate territory, male, female, gay, straight, married, single, or whatever, brain-washed by different upbringings and prejudices. However liberal we each previously thought our-selves, we were now face to face with 'the others' and so many preconceptions were proving to be wrong. It would be easy to satirise this part of the workshop as a sixties hippy encounter group, but I think we were experiencing something valuable, exchanging prejudice for knowledge.
>
> (Ritchie 1987: 139–40)

Sher certainly felt that he learned to appreciate other points of view and came to appreciate feminist concerns. But the real problem, 'the most disastrous part of the Joint Stock structure', he has argued, was the break between the workshop and the rehearsal period while the play was being written, during which time the actors were 'unpaid and half-committed' and 'the idealism of the workshop was quickly corrupted into a paranoia about what the actual written play, and crucially, the *parts* would be like' (Ritchie 1987: 140).

Churchill was able to deliver only Act I by the deadline: set in a British colony in Africa during the height of the Victorian empire, the geographical and historical location was not at all what the actors were expecting. As Sher saw it: 'Caryl had obviously been inspired and encouraged by the workshop, but had then taken a bold imaginative leap and used a different period and society to highlight the themes of sexual prejudice and role-playing' (Ritchie 1987: 141). Rehearsals began, 'the group chemistry mysteriously evaporating', with Churchill in part attendance, but also disappearing to write Act II (Ritchie 1987: 141). Churchill delivered a second act set in 1970s' London, historically a century later but with characters who had only aged 25 years. No one was much persuaded by it; Stafford-Clark feared 'disaster round the corner' and was not convinced he had a play; Sher noted astutely that it was a much easier task 'dealing with a reactionary society [Act I] than a liberated one [Act II]' (Roberts and Stafford-Clark 2007: 92–93). Otherwise, actors felt that since they had exposed their own lives they should have more ownership of material and choice over parts (*Plays 1* 1985: 89). Churchill was under intense pressure, and Margolyes ruminated that 'perhaps we wanted the play to deliver the rounded conclusions to our own lives which we were so signally unable to provide to ourselves' (*Plays 1* 1985: 89). Rehearsals were therefore tense and bad-tempered, the actors feeling disappointed in their roles and minimised in importance. The fragmented accounts record turmoil and panic among the cast but one of the reasons for *Cloud Nine's* success is that it did confront sexual politics in provocative and personal ways. That turmoil was not just confined to its original making: rehearsals of the American premiere also caused intense debate among its American cast who found themselves painfully challenged by the material, and registered 'hostility' and 'outrage' as well as concern for how their friends and family would react (Thurman 1982: 57). As it turned out, New York audiences could not have been more appreciative.

Representing sex and gender

There is more critical and theoretical disagreement about the status and possible meanings of performances of *Cloud Nine* than any other play by Churchill. A production directed by Tom Cairns at London's

Old Vic in 1997, which formed part of Peter Hall's season of modern classics, drew a characteristic spectrum of opinion from reviewers. James Treadwell of the *Spectator* found it 'thought-provoking, extremely funny, absolutely compelling'; Brian Logan in *Time Out* described it as 'dated, comically naive, crude'; Charles Spencer in the *Daily Telegraph* felt positively threatened, perceiving it to be 'tendentious, man-hating, actively malign'; and Paul Taylor in the *Independent* extolled the exploration of 'liberation politics' in play and production as 'genuinely liberating'.[6] Academic theorists have been polarised, arguing either that Churchill's play demonstrates an entrenched sexual conservatism or that it presents an iconoclastic critique of gender production and the structures of representation.

The most hotly disputed subjects of *Cloud Nine* are Churchill's time-and-location split narrative and her experimentation with cross-sex casting. Act I is set at the height of the British Empire in an unspecified African country in 1879, and Act II is located in London in 1979. Act I presents the family of colonial administrator Clive, his wife Betty, their son Edward and daughter Victoria, and Betty's mother Maud. The domestic circle includes Ellen, Edward's governess, Joshua, the family's black servant, and two visitors – an explorer, Harry Bagley, and a widow, Mrs Saunders. Churchill rationalised Act I as a device to show the historical context to changing sexual attitudes in 1970s' Britain. It was needed, she argued:

> in order to show the sorts of changes people felt they'd had to make. When we discussed our backgrounds it occurred to us it was as if everyone felt they had been born almost in the Victorian age. Everyone had grown up with quite conventional and old-fashioned expectations about sex and marriage and felt that they themselves had had to make enormous break-aways and leaps to change their lives from that.
>
> (Truss 1984: 10)

In Act I, Churchill exposes the chasm between repressive Victorian conventions of gendered social behaviours and her characters' primal sexual desires. Thus Clive is the imperial patriarch, 'father' to family and natives (slaves) (*Plays 1* 1985: 251), preaching duty and sexual restraint and believing in queen, country and the mission to 'civilise'; yet at the same time he is indulging in a wanton sexual affair with Mrs Saunders whom he wishes to conquer and territorialise: 'You are dark like this continent' (*Plays 1* 1985: 263). His wife Betty is played by a man to highlight the fact that she has no identity or visibility as a woman in her own right: 'I live for Clive. The whole aim of my life is to be what he looks for in a wife' (*Plays 1* 1985: 251); but actually Betty longs for an affair with Harry. Edward, played by a woman, tries to conform to his father's expectations of masculinity but prefers playing with his sister's doll, indulging in secret sex with Harry, and does nothing to warn Clive of the impending danger when Joshua raises his gun to shoot him at the end of Act I. Victoria, who has even less identity and visibility than her mother, is simply a dummy, who is praised, scolded or hit according to others' whims. Ellen's lesbianism, although declared (she is in love with Betty), goes completely unrecognised and she is married off to Harry both to fulfil her duty as a wife and mother in the empire, and, although she does not know it, to quell her new husband's homosexuality. Maud knows only duty, restraint, self-denial and self-imposed ignorance: 'Clive will know what to do. Your father always knew what to do' (*Plays 1* 1985: 274). A widow, Mrs Saunders is treated as defenceless and dependent by Clive, but is bold, politically dissident, sexually forthright and regards marriage as a sham; a further theatrical irony is effected through the doubling of Ellen's part with Mrs Saunders. The servant, Joshua, is black but played by a white actor, and is apparently obedient to Clive: 'What white men want is what I want to be' (*Plays 1* 1985: 252); yet he defies Betty's orders, informs against her, and eventually turns on his master. Churchill's cross-sex casting and the revelation of 'illegitimate' private desires become devices for exposing the transgression of strict social and sexual codes: order is merely an illusion, anarchy is the psychic reality that symbolically culminates in Joshua's violent rebellion against Clive.

The disjuncture between actor and character is rendered yet more complex by the discontinuity between Act I and Act II: a century has passed but the characters have only aged 25 years. In Act II actors play entirely different parts, thus offering up different doublings to scrutiny. In 1970s' Britain Clive has disappeared altogether, although not the actor who played him (who in the premiere played Cathy, Lin's four-year-old daughter – the only piece of cross-sex casting in Act II). Betty (now played by a female actor who had another role in Act I) has discovered that masturbation is permissible, joyous and does not have to be guilt-ridden; she has also begun her first job. Lin (an 'outed' version of Ellen from Act I) and Victoria initially form a lesbian alliance and then a threesome with Edward (also Victoria's brother). Martin, Victoria's husband (who has echoes of Clive's character), argues for liberated relationships but seems unable to relinquish the desire to control his wife and cannot give her sexual pleasure. Gerry is repulsed by Edward's desire for domestic control and experiences freedom through casual sexual encounters with men. In the last scene, Betty attempts to pick up Gerry mistakenly assuming he is heterosexual; she also accepts that her son is 'gay' although he also sleeps with women. An unreconstructed Clive momentarily appears, laments the loss of empire and refuses to accept what Betty has become. The final image is a striking tableau of Betty from Act I and Betty from Act II locked in an embrace, which suggests that Betty is moving towards becoming an integrated, expressive sexual subject freed from previous codes of repression and control.

Double trouble

In her production notes, Churchill is clear that the cross-sex casting of Betty, Edward and Cathy is non-negotiable, as is the casting of a white male actor to play Joshua. Apart from this, 'doubling can be done in any way that seems right for any particular production' and sets up 'some interesting resonances between the two acts' (*Plays 1* 1985: 247). *Cloud Nine*, then, has built-in representationally reflexive mechanisms for revealing the production of history as a patriarchal narrative, and for exposing the production of gender and the manufacture of mandated social appearances versus desire. The theoretical disputes have been centred on whether Churchill is successful in seeking new representational forms, new strategies for encoding the body and new ways of organising sex/gender relations, as theorists such as Silverstein (1994) have argued, or whether she is simply reinforcing hetero-patriarchal frameworks as Harding (1998) has asserted.

Both Silverstein and Harding borrow ideas about gender construction from theorist Judith Butler, whose writings on sex and gender formation, notably in her book *Gender Trouble* (1990), offer ways of seeing *Cloud Nine*.[7] Building on Simone de Beauvoir's famous statement 'One is not born a woman, one becomes one',[8] Butler argues that heterosexual, heterosexist cultures have established the exclusive binary tyranny of the categories 'man' and 'woman', 'male' and 'female' to perpetuate a dominant order in which men and women are required, or even forced, to be heterosexual. According to Butler,

> 'woman' itself is a term in process, a becoming, a constructing that cannot rightfully be said to originate or end. As an ongoing discursive practice, it is open to intervention and resignification.
>
> (Butler 1990a: 33)

It is the task of feminist critique, Butler argues, 'to understand how the category of "women", the subject of feminism is produced and restrained by the very structures of power through which emancipation is sought' (Butler 1990a: 2). Sex and gender are cultural constructions that define and construct the body, and gender dissonance or 'gender trouble' can be deployed to highlight that gender is a fictive production. For Butler gender is 'performatively produced and compelled by regulatory practices of gender coherence', and sex is produced by gender. The very performance of gender, therefore, constitutes the identity it purports to express. 'In this sense gender is always a doing, though not a doing by a subject who might be said to pre-exist the deed' (Butler 1990a: 25). In her essay 'Performative Acts and Gender Constitution' Butler endeavours to think through her theory of gender construction in relation to the specificity of theatre. If identity is a performative construction it is:

> tenuously constituted in time – an identity instituted through a stylised repetition of acts. Further, gender is instituted through the stylisation of the body and, hence, must be understood as the mundane way in which bodily gestures, movements and enactments of various kinds constitute the illusion of an abiding gendered self [...] This repetition is at once a reenactment and a re-experiencing of a set of meanings already socially established; it is the mundane and ritualised form of their legitimation.
>
> (Butler 1990b: 270, 277)

Butler's theorisation that gender is created through iterative performance lends itself well to the sexual codifications of Act I. Binary definitions of sexuality are so strictly enforced that the rejection of heterosexual codes of female behaviour is conceivable but not possible, and these disjunctive eruptions provide many of the farcical moments. The female body appears only as an object of male desire. Maud and Betty have moulded themselves most readily and have voluntarily yielded autonomy. Ellen's lesbianism has no legitimacy, and cannot come into being because the others are unable to recognise it. Until Victoria reaches puberty and can be traded in the sexual marketplace she effectively has no existence as a female, and is represented as a doll. Mrs Saunders' waywardness is voiced but she has no effective route to transform her frustration into a power-base of resistance. Joshua might be a slave but as a black male is more visible than the white women and it is significant that he initiates a revolutionary moment. In Act II the sexual spectrum has broadened and, symbolically, the dominant patriarch, Clive, is absent. Churchill has written that the first act was designed to be 'male dominated and firmly structured', and that the 'looser structure' of the second act conveyed 'a less authoritarian feeling' (*Plays 1* 1985: 246). Different gender constructions of female heterosexuality, lesbianism and bisexuality have become legitimate and can be performed in public spheres. Cathy, in particular, the child played by a man, demonstrates that gender is influenced by environment. But characters are confused rather than liberated; they invent and reinvent their sexuality in relation to others and from situation to situation, and their sex and genders match Butler's processual model rather than presenting any fixity. In *Cloud Nine*, Silverstein argues, Churchill has formulated a utopian experiment, exploring 'an alternative representation economy in which opposition to patriarchal power relations could express itself', and in so doing she contests 'patriarchal structures at the level of cultural representation itself' (Silverstein 1994: 13–14). Harding, on the other hand, has argued that Churchill's representation of lesbian and gay characters assumes that 'the presumption of heterosexuality always serves as the foundation for any new social context' and that supposedly transgressive moments such as Ellen's and Harry's kiss at the end of Act I 'repeatedly function as a means of sidestepping homoerotic enactments' – in this instance because though the characters are lesbian and gay, the actors are male and female and thus a heterosexual encounter is represented: 'the categories on which the inversions rely inscribe gay men and lesbians into heterosexuality as a matter of course' (Harding 1998: 266, 271). Harding asserts that the truth sessions in the workshop phase represented an advance that the play later conceded:

> the autobiographical 'truth sessions' of the workshop made the actors' sexual identities visible in a way that they were not in the later performances. The sessions thus facilitated a Brechtian alienation of actors and characters along the lines not merely of gender but of sexual orientation as well.
>
> (Harding 1998: 266)

Today, Out of Joint's experiments appear naïve. Casting on the basis of sexual orientation seems an essentialist exercise, and the workshop improvisations were essentialist in trying to identify masculine and feminine characteristics (Roberts and Stafford-Clark 2007: 76). Harding's arguments that homosexual and lesbian practices cannot be rendered legible by simple inversions of the categories of man and woman, and that Churchill's stated preferences for doubling reinforces a heterosexual matrix, are compelling. In Butler's model it is hard to see how progress might be made without constant and concerted assertion of alternative gender constructions – more varied constructions than Churchill's Act II provides. In fact, Churchill's historical exploration in *Cloud Nine* seems most focused on change for heterosexual women, and her image of the two Bettys embracing at the end of the play reinforces this idea. Betty's ability to experience guiltless orgasms marks her independence from others and her self-discovery is moving: 'I felt triumphant because I was a separate person' (*Plays 1* 1985: 316). *Cloud Nine* can and has been appropriated to promote conservative sexual agendas. For the American premiere director Tommy Tune had seen the Royal Court production and wanted spectators to be absolutely clear that they had 'permission to laugh' in Act I (although one of the traps of *Cloud Nine* is that the farce is all too easily camped up). He also demanded a 'more uplifting ending' and moved Betty's monologue about finally experiencing an orgasm to the end of the play (Betsko and Koenig 1987: 83). Betty thus became a tragic protagonist depicted at the end of a journey and not *en route* or, to use Butler's formulation, 'in process'. Tune played to Broadway sentimentalism and to the strictures of a hetero-patriarchal narrative: Betty abandoned her submissive past but was punished by being isolated. Given Churchill's critique of the scape-goating and marginalisation of older women in *Vinegar Tom*, this modification was more than a little ironic. In Churchill's words:

> The effect was that the whole thing reached a much more emotional climax. It also made it more American, in that it made it more about an individual's self-development and rather less about the society and the group of people. It worried me a bit, but I could see that it worked.
>
> (Truss 1984: 9)

In the twenty-first century, Butler's theory too has dated, and, in any case, seemed ill-at-ease with the physical fact of the body in perfor-mance. The relation between biology, gender identity and sexual orientation is no longer assumed to be straightforward. Current research shows that transgenderism has 'replaced homosexuality as the newest civil-right frontier' in America;[9] gender switching occurs at younger and younger ages, and as Talbot has argued: 'Transpeople are increasingly choosing to place themselves somewhere between male and female: [...] styling their appearance in gender-confounding ways but abstaining from medical procedures.'[10] Sexuality and gender are far more fluid concepts than they were in the 1970s. So has *Cloud Nine* become the history play that its first director, Max Stafford-Clark, fears it may be in danger of becoming?

> Twenty years on, Caryl's brilliant capturing of our own hippy-go-lucky self-involvement had become as quaint and distant as the repressed mores of the repressed Victorians. The first half had always been a history play, but our endeavour to articulate our own sexual confusion had become history too in the inter-vening years.
>
> (Roberts and Stafford-Clark 2007: 96).

There is a far more serious problem with productions of *Cloud Nine* and a far more serious problem with most theorists who have written on it, and that is the blind-spot in relation to its racial politics. Churchill's 'Africa' is a literary construct designed to expose sexual stereotypes, but it is also a blunt instrument that totally erases questions of ethnicity. Churchill has spoken of the constraint of writing for a white cast (Thurman 1982: 57) and expressed interest in a suggestion that a black actor might play Harry Bagley.[11] This would not answer Harding's concerns, nor would it answer third wave feminist theorist Apollo Amoko's damning attack on those who 'appear to use colonial and racial difference to produce social and critical authority for westernised notions of gender and sexual difference', and who have concentrated on feminist agendas to 'the near total exclusion of any in-depth or sustained examination of race and colonialism' (Amoko 1999: 45–46). Churchill's post-workshop decision to set Act I in 'Africa' did not result in any recasting on the basis of ethnicity, and that decision must be questioned.

Cloud Nine is long overdue for creative reinvention by directors who want to experiment with cross-racial casting. Non-white characters vanish altogether in Act II, which is a serious flaw. Depressingly, it still tends to be treated only as a canvas to investigate cross-sex casting and the inherent prejudices of continuing to ignore ethnic agendas and the failure to expose those politics and produce new meanings cannot be overlooked. If, as Lee Lewis argues, 'theatre is a constructor of future class, of future race relations, and ultimately of the imagined future national identity, then a production can be shaped to persuade an audience to think in a particular way about a play's message' (Lewis 2007: 22). The Arts Council 2001 *Eclipse Report* on the racist structures of much British theatre revealed the 'cultural face of an imperial politics of domination' (Lewis 2007: 54), and demonstrated that diverse casting was not being advanced because of the attitudes of artistic directors and directors who did not perceive that they were prejudiced.[12] One can only imagine that Caryl Churchill would like to see advances here too. Indeed, now that the non-white population of London is larger (55.1 per cent) than the white share (44.9 per cent), as the results of the 2011 census demonstrate, it seems very odd that more progress by theatre companies has not been made. In the words of Lewis:

As plays present their embedded value-systems and their perspectives on how the world is or should be, so productions present versions of these values embodied by the actors, selected by the directors. Directors are selecting the bodies with which to present ideas bearing on the future: they are offering a physical vision of the future for the audience to accept or reject, and seeking to influence that choice [...] Failure to implement diverse casting now is likely to cause people to imagine a continuing segregation in the future. [...] exclusion risks creating far worse social problems by constructing an imagined White community as a national ideal for the future.

(Lewis 2007: 23)

In Britain *Cloud Nine* is still waiting for a director and theatre company to step forward and offer a new imagining; indeed, it remains to be seen *if* it can hold up to alternative racial imaginings.

Notes

1 See the documentary, *Omnibus: Caryl Churchill*, BBC 1, 4 November 1988.
2 Sources disagree. Antony Sher in Ritchie (1987) and Roberts (2008), for example, list different constituencies but all include gays, lesbians and heterosexual men and women.
3 Public interview of Max Stafford-Clark by Mary Luckhurst, Dixon Studio, University of York, 8 December 2004.
4 Both have a tendency to speak on behalf of the group.
5 His solution was to leave quotations unattributed.
6 James Treadwell, the *Spectator*, 29 March 1997; Brian Logan, *Time Out*, 26 March 1997; Charles Spencer, *The Daily Telegraph*, 25 March 1997; Paul Taylor, *The Independent*, 22 March 1997.
7 For other landmark works see Tom Laqueur, *Making Sex: Body and Gender from the Greeks to Freud* (Cambridge, MA: Harvard, 1990) and Pat Caplan, *The Cultural Construction of Sexuality* (London: Routledge, 1987).
8 See Simone de Beauvoir, *The Second Sex* (New York: Vintage, 1973).
9 Margaret Talbot, 'About a Boy', *The New Yorker*, March 18 2013: 56.
10 Margaret Talbot, 'About a Boy', *The New Yorker*, March 18 2013: 62.
11 See Laurie Stone, *The Village Voice*, 1 March 1983: 80–81.
12 Stuart Brown, *Eclipse Report: Developing Strategies to Combat Racism in Theatre* (London: Arts Council, 2001).

Part III

Thatcherism, the New Right and the 1980s

5   Key Production: *Top Girls*

The Britain of the 1980s has become synonymous with the premiership of the so-called Iron Lady, Margaret Thatcher (1979–90), the New Right, the ideology of entrepreneurial individualism, and the polarity of extravagant consumption versus the struggle of the poor and unemployed. Churchill's *Top Girls*, sometimes referred to as her 'Thatcher play', is reflective of its era (Milling 2012), and in 2013 Benedict Nightingale listed it as among the 20 most influential plays in theatre history, stating that 'no playwright, male or female, has proved more daringly imaginative'.[1] Thatcherism stood for everything that Churchill, then a socialist feminist, deplored. Although a role model as Britain's first woman prime minister, Thatcher denied that feminism had done anything for her at her first press conference, identifying with a world of conservative masculinity as she was to do throughout her regime.[2]

An advocate of Milton Friedman's theory of monetarism (Friedman 1962), Thatcher privileged the free market economy and embarked on privatising public industries and deregulating government services. The New Right believed the welfare state fostered a parasitic dependency culture that impeded personal initiative and individual responsibility: indeed, Thatcher became notorious for announcing 'There is no such thing as society' and referring to the poor as 'drooling and driveling'.[3] The proper scope of public and private provision became a key issue (as it remains today). Thatcher's government began dismantling the public sector on an unprecedented scale and privatisation became part of an ideological drive towards popular capitalism.[4] Borrowing Friedman's rhetoric of 'freedom' and 'choice', Thatcher disabled the trades unions, reduced welfare benefits and increased the private markets in health and education. Left-wing political theorist Stuart Hall wrote passionately about the break with the post-1945 economic consensus:

> One after another the old landmarks – full employment, welfare state support, equality of opportunity, the 'caring' society, neo-Keynesian economic management, corporatist incomes policies – have been reversed. In their place a new public philosophy has been constructed, rooted in the open affirmation of 'free market values' – the market as the measure of everything – and reactionary 'Victorian' social values – patriarchalism, racism and imperialist nostalgia. The whole shift towards a more authoritarian type of regime has been grounded in the search for 'Order' and the cry for 'Law' which arises among many ordinary people in times of crisis and upheaval.
>
> (Hall and Jacques 1983: 13)

Thatcher's battle against the miners in 1984 became symbolic of her campaign to end the government-subsidised industrial base, and significant numbers in the north lost their jobs as pits were closed and communities abandoned to deprivation and poverty. The division of wealth between the north and south of England became a sensitive political issue, by 1985 3.2 million people were unemployed, and in 1990 Thatcher was forced to resign because her policies had alienated the majority. Hall, like many commentators, found monetarism to be an inherently divisive political model, mass unemployment a permanent feature: 'at the bottom the permanently unemployed and the marginals, dependent on falling welfare entitlements; in the middle the regularly employed, increasingly divided by enterprise, sector and hierarchy; at the top, the increasing wealth and income of capitalists and top managers' (Hall and Jacques 1983: 15).

Explorations of these economic and social divides permeate Churchill's best-known work in the 1980s. *Top Girls* investigates working women across the economic spectrum in an era when authors such as Shirley Conran were polemicising that the modern go-getting woman could have an executive career, material wealth and the perfect domestic life. The watchword for Conran's bestseller *Superwoman* (1975) was that 'women could have it all,' and that everything could be juggled without sacrifice. Celebrating the brazen sexuality of Madonna's pop videos and Joan Collins' ruthless Alexis in *Dynasty*, Conran and her followers proclaimed that 'no self-respecting woman could afford scruples in the race to get ahead'.[5] The apex of success was the 'yuppie',[6] a 1980s neologism for the phenomenon of get-rich-quick city professionals and Sloane Rangers, famed for immoderate consumption. Marlene in *Top Girls* is defined by yuppie aspirations, and the characters in *Serious Money* (1987), Churchill's hit about the cynical, exploitative culture among financiers working London's stock market, are ciphers for the greed and profligacy driving the capitalist engine. *Fen* (1983) frames rural poverty against global capitalism and examines the alienation and despair brought about by state neglect. *Softcops* (1984), Churchill's only creative partnership with the Royal Shakespeare Company, and inspired by Foucault's *Discipline and Punish* (1977), interrogates state control, policing and punishment, drawing clear lines between poverty, social disadvantage and crime. But it is *Top Girls* that has become the signature play of the 1980s, and one of the most celebrated modern plays in the world.

The genesis of *Top Girls*

Top Girls was directed by Max Stafford-Clark and premiered at the Royal Court Theatre in 1982. It transferred to the Joseph Papp Theatre in New York and returned to London in February 1983. More than any other of her plays, *Top Girls* reminds us that Churchill's artistic enterprise has not just been about challenging form, but is fundamentally concerned with representing that rather rare thing on modern stages – a spectrum of non-stereotypical women from different classes and generations. Churchill has written some of the most provocative parts for actresses in modern theatre, and the contrasting multiple roles offered in *Top Girls* have made it an irresistible challenge for many performers.

The idea for *Top Girls* was seeded by a trip to America and Churchill's encounter with a more right-wing feminism that prompted her to think about the differences between socialist agendas in Europe and individualist neo-liberalism in the USA (Truss 1984: 9). Characteristically, Churchill was also attracted by breaking a golden rule of playwriting – the need to keep a realistic cap on the numbers of parts: 'My original idea was to write a play for an enormous number of women, and I just wrote a play that had six-teen women's parts in it' (Truss 1984: 10). The large cast proved financially unviable, but Churchill kept the 16 roles and in the pre-miere six of the seven actresses played multiple parts. *Top Girls* was and is a departure from the norm simply in the range and ambition of its female roles, and at the time it was rare in its depiction of representing contemporary women in the workplace.

Stafford-Clark has spoken of Margaret Thatcher as the 'starting-point' for the play,[7] and Churchill was clear that Thatcher's politics spurred her writing:

> Thatcher had just become prime minister; there was talk about whether it was an advance to have a woman PM if it was someone with policies like hers: she may be a woman but she isn't a sister, she may be a sister but she isn't a comrade. And, in fact, things have got much worse for women under Thatcher. [...] Of course, socialism and feminism aren't synonymous, but I feel strongly about both and wouldn't be interested in a form of one that didn't include the other. [...] What I was intending to do in *Top Girls* was make it first look as though it was cele-brating the achievements of women and then – by showing the main character, Marlene, being successful in a very competitive, destructive, capitalist way – ask what kind of achievement is that? The idea was that it would start out looking like a feminist play and turn into a socialist one [...] women are pressured to make choices between working and having children in a way that men aren't.
>
> (Betsko and Koenig 1987: 82)

At the American premiere, Marlene's bouffant hair and blue suits ensured that critics saw much more than Thatcher's influence and read Marlene, the central character, as a caricature of Thatcher herself.[8] Churchill's influences for the play can also be located in her interest in biography and her search for inspiration from remark-able women of the past; in her discussions and workshops with the female collectives Monstrous Regiment and Women in Entertain-ment; and in her interview research for *Top Girls* at an employment agency where she was inspired by what Stafford-Clark described as 'a buccaneering spirit'[9] (Roberts 2008: 207–11).

Exploding plot and form

With *Top Girls*, Churchill pushed her experiments with plot and form further than ever: she originally wrote three acts with intervals in between to highlight the separateness of each act, but there were fears that the evening would become too prolonged (*Plays 2* 1990: 54). Stafford-Clark saw it as 'three separate plays, requiring three different paces and styles of performance'.[10] The play's form requires spectators to travel backwards in time and, as a result, information is withheld in ways that gradually bring a new, darker perspective to Marlene's successful career. Act III takes place a year before Marlene's riotous celebration of her promotion to managing director at the Top Girls employment agency in Act I, and before Act II at Marlene's office in London; it exposes the emotional and financial abandonment of her daughter, Angie, and of her sister, Joyce, who has struggled to raise Angie as her own child. Marlene has left her rural, working-class life and reinvented herself as a city slicker, but is in denial that she is a mother at all, and has no plans to help Angie or Joyce improve their lives or to include them in her own. To Marlene the very existence of her daughter and sister is a cancerous secret that can have no part in her reconstructed life. Indeed, Angie and Joyce represent an invisible class of women – downtrodden, forgotten and without opportunity. A star at the beginning, Marlene appears ruthless, self-absorbed and unethical by the end.

If capitalism is predicated on the exploitation of the impoverished and disempowered, is it possible for successful women in capitalist societies to avoid becoming complicit in oppression? What might be sacrificed in order to achieve success? Should women ask questions about how 'success' is defined? For Churchill these are central questions in *Top Girls*, and she embeds them into the play through structural shifts of perspective that initially disorient spectators but effectively coerce them into re-examining their responses to Marlene at the end of the evening. The stylistic and aesthetic explosion that happens between Act I and Act II has intrigued successive generations of playwrights, and *Top Girls'* legacy is clear in plays such as *Mother Clap's Molly House* by Mark Ravenhill and *Blasted* by Sarah Kane.[11] Marlene is the significant plot connection between the three acts and, unlike the other members of the cast, the actress in this role does not play any other parts. Formally, the collective

chaos of Act I is mirrored by Angie's mental vulnerability and isolation at the end of Act III: terrified by a nightmare, she seeks con-
solation from Marlene who is singularly unresponsive both to her
daughter's cries of 'Mum?' and to her neediness. For Stafford-Clark
the ending sounded a warning of what was to come:

> The moment when Angie says 'frightening' is [...] frighteningly
> prophetic, written on the threshold of Thatcher's eighties, as it
> posits the perspective that those who are less talented, those
> who are weaker will go to the wall. Of course that is what
> happened.
>
> (Roberts 2008: 217)

The staging and performance challenges presented by Act I's *coup
de théâtre* are celebrated: the whole of the act is a dinner hosted
by Marlene in which multiple narratives clash and overlap. The
guests are historical figures brought to life or fictional. Besides
Marlene, only the waitress is living and contemporaneous. The
restaurant dinner served and consumed in real-time is one of
the most extraordinary conceits in modern drama, described at the
time as 'beyond daring' by the American theatre critic Frank Rich.[12]
The characters have nothing of the air of ghosts, their gradual collapse into drunken, chaotic discord lending them a peculiar charge.
These historical and fictional characters appear only in Act I and
function as the equivalent of a long lens through which to view the
present-day situation for women. For the actors, the scene has
become a notorious test of their professionalism: eating the meal,
performing gradual intoxication, maintaining character and timing
the complicated overlapping speech require significant skill and
concentration. For the director, the challenge is to create the
sophisticated choreography required by the text, to find the dyna-
mism and comedy of the clashing discourses, to ensure that the
audience can see and hear the detail of the action (not easy when
actresses are seated most of the time and often talking across each
other), and to find the slow acceleration into chaotic drunkeness.
For the premiere Stafford-Clark was concerned that the first act
made too many demands on the audience, and that the fragmented
narratives might bewilder rather than seduce, but at the first pre-
view his anxieties were completely stilled[13]: in his diary he noted

Figure 5.1 Stella Gonet, Laura Elphinstone, Olivia Poulet, Lucy Briers, Suranne Jones and Catherine McCormack in *Top Girls*, Trafalgar
Studios, London © John Haynes

'Best play I've ever directed. How quickly the audience accepts a
surreal convention' (Roberts 2008: 210).

Marlene's invited guests include Isabella Bird, an intrepid Victorian explorer, natural historian and woman of letters; Lady Nijo,
a Japanese emperor's concubine from the thirteenth century who
later wrote her memoirs and became a Buddhist nun; Pope Joan,
allegedly a learned woman who disguised herself as a man, becoming the pope before being exposed by childbirth and suffering a
violent death;[14] Patient Griselda, a figure from folklore chronicled
by Boccaccio, Petrarch and Chaucer who showed inexplicable and
unwavering obedience to the cruel trials inflicted on her by her tyr-
annical husband; and Dull Gret, a figure from Flemish folklore
(famously painted by Pieter Breughel the Elder in 1526), who led an
army of women in an attack on hell. It seems no coincidence that
Churchill's two real-life women selected from the past, Bird and
Nijo, were writers and are remembered for their writing.

The dinner party guests, 'social victims as well as pioneers',
exchange their stories (Billington 2009: 307): what they share is the
impossibility or terrible struggle of becoming the authors of their

own lives, the serious prohibitions and abuses imposed on them by patriarchal structures of power, and often the death, loss or removal of their children. Set against these narratives Churchill intended Marlene to stand out as the 'feminist heroine who had done things against extraordinary odds' (Roberts 2008: 214). The whole act serves to highlight that all are survivors of brutalising, misogynistic worlds but that the sharing of their individual trauma is not enough to provide the bridge to mutual understanding. In fact, the guests at the dinner party do not share the same values or the same views although, ironically, all conspire in the marginalisation of the wait- ress. As we realise later, the telling absences at the table are Angie and Joyce, and the telling silence is Marlene's personal history. Through her character choices at the dinner Churchill foregrounds the complexity of cultural and historical differences and of ideological strangleholds, the varying life/death risks implicated in resistance, the cultural variation of opportunity to resist oppression, and the subjective difference in personal levels of stamina and courage. Implicitly, the act foreshadows a terrain that postcolonial feminist theorists would shortly investigate for themselves.[15]

Actresses on performing *Top Girls* in the twenty-first century

Stafford-Clark revived *Top Girls* in 1991 at the National Theatre, and again in 2011 at the Chichester Theatre, the Trafalgar Studios in London and, with a different cast, for a touring production in 2012. This section examines accounts by actresses involved in Stafford-Clark's most recent revivals in relation to the opinions expressed by actresses about the premiere in 1982; such a compar- ison is an enlightening exercise because it allows us to consider the ways in which performers' viewpoints towards the roles, the subject matter and the technical challenges of the play have shifted signficantly over 30 years.

The precision demanded by Act I is no less demanding today than it was for the premiere production. Churchill advised casts for the 2011/12 revivals on the exact points at which overlaps should begin or end, as she had done in 1982. Lesley Manville, who acted in the premiere, has described the overlapping dialogue as 'horrendously difficult', not just in terms of line-learning but timing the precise moment for interruption. She has also talked about the performance possibilities offered by the scene's ever-shifting multiple points of focus:

> Rehearsing with overlapping dialogue means that instead of having somebody speaking and then passing the baton to the next character who speaks, you can have a lot more throwaway dialogue, and of course it isn't all important. With the overlapping, you can rehearse in such a way that [the question becomes]: 'who do we want the audience to look at?' It's not just a question of who speaks loudest; it's a question of passing the baton successfully so that the audience have some of the work done for them.
>
> (Roberts 2008: 215–16)

Olivia Poulet, who performed in Chichester and the West End in 2011, notes that, although other playwrights (notably Martin Crimp) have experimented with overlaps, none have been as radical as Churchill. Poulet is intrigued by the sensory overload deliberately imposed on audience members by the construction of the text and argues that Churchill is interested in altering the spectator's usual state of receptivity. Critics might describe the scene as a 'fantasia' but she insists that 'as actors we think of ourselves as real women at a real dinner party in real time – a steep performance challenge'.

> The dinner scene is a symphony of sound, with sections that seem particularly cacophonous, and I was amazed by the clarity Caryl could bring when she asked for a slight pause or a particular emphasis on a single word. It was as though she was marking a score and could hear all the vocal instruments sounding through. You have to let the scene wash over you as an audience member: if you worry or become frustrated that you are not catching every word or action you will not absorb the effect of the scene. When we get it exactly to time it works brilliantly. No other playwright has done overlaps to the same extent as Caryl and I find that interesting – it's a testament to her mastery. She's a genius.[16]

The differences of opinion between casts in relation to Marlene are especially revealing. In the 1982 production, the cast found

Marlene difficult to like. Manville found it hard to tolerate Marlene's Thatcherism, egotism and greed, and was very conscious of the gap between her own personal politics and Marlene's political credo (Roberts 2008: 212–13). Stafford-Clark advised his actresses to 'dig deep [...] to find the pain' (Roberts 2008: 210). As a result, Deborah Findlay – who played Joyce – made Marlene palatable through finding a rather saintly selflessness in Joyce's decision to care for Angie and she became persuaded of a deep love between the sisters. 'I think Joyce loves Marlene very much, and Marlene loves Joyce very much' (Roberts 2008: 212). By contrast, the actresses in the 2011/12 revivals professed a much greater sympathy and understanding for Marlene, even though they saw the relationship between the sisters as destructive. Suranne Jones, who performed Marlene in Chichester and London, was as concerned about Marlene's treatment of herself as her abuse of others:

> I understand why Marlene felt she had to leave her family and her childhood behind her, but my sympathy is seriously tested by the fact that she abandoned her own child in the process. I think the structure of the play allows you to understand why Marlene treats Angie and Joyce as she does, reveals the damage to herself, and the cost of her actions to the three of them.[17]

Olivia Poulet, who played opposite Jones as Angie, saw Marlene as a tough, independent political pragmatist:

> Through the representation of Marlene and her sister we get to see both perspectives – this is an enormously clever piece of parallel construction. I don't sympathise with Marlene's Tory politics – however, when she says that if you come from nothing you have to create your own success, I believe she is right. She's single-minded, determined and ambitious; no one makes the opportunities for you, you have to go out and fight. A lot of women identify with that now.[18]

Caroline Catz, who played Marlene in the 2012 touring production and had wanted to perform in *Top Girls* since reading it,[19] was unequivocal in her assessment of Marlene as 'the best role I've ever played'.[20] In interview she noted that powerful, autonomous roles for women are a rarity and that she could flex muscles that she is not normally invited to do:

> It's so liberating to play a woman who will not let herself be defined by men. As I see it, Marlene's narcissism, which was found unacceptable in the 1980s, is the very thing that younger women in the 21st century understand as a given in the battle to succeed at work. It is shocking, however, when Marlene says of Angie ' she's not going to make it'. It's so much more of a betrayal for a mother to give up on her own daughter and condemn her to a refuse heap. It's an indictment of class and gender politics in England that for Marlene to admit to emotional connection with her sister and daughter is to threaten all she has achieved. It's not too late for Angie, it's never too late. Marlene's philosophy is that you make your own way – but without her sister's generosity where would she be? The truth is, you need the break and Joyce gave Marlene the break she needed but Marlene only seems to despise her for it.[21]

These appraisals suggest that in 1982 Marlene's rejection of a domestic, nurturing role and refusal to acknowledge the responsibility of motherhood were perceived as dangerously transgressive. Marlene's insistence on privileging career above domestic politics rendered her something of a villain to the cast and her right-wing politics only increased her disapproval rating. The reactions from the casts in 2011/12 indicate that performers had a more nuanced appreciation of the career-versus-family dilemma, and of the sacrifices and conflicts either one or both routes might entail. The fact that careers for women are unquestionably affected by childbearing is evident in the statistical rise for late motherhood – women who wait until after they are 35 before they have their first child are now a social phenomenon in many Western democracies.[22] Marlene no longer seems to induce anxiety and disapproval among casts, indeed, for all her flaws she inspires a certain admiration and recognition. Actresses positively revel in her gutsiness, professionalism and refusal to make compromises, and now feel permitted to take pleasure in playing Marlene while not making excuses for her. Interestingly, Churchill decided that Marlene was Angie's mother at a late stage in the drafting of the play, and has said that Marlene's abandonment of Angie 'isn't the main point' (Roberts 2008: 211). Despite Churchill's intention, Marlene is still judged more by her treatment of her own child than by anything else (including her treatment of her sister and other women at work). It seems absent fathers can be accounted for by a recognisable sociological category but absent mothers are still an offence against nature.[23]

Reactions to the role of Angie also provide an interesting touchstone. In 1982 Deborah Findlay (Joyce) and Gwen Taylor (Marlene) based much of their performance on an improvisation in which they discussed who would raise the baby and their feelings about it. This presumed 'an enormous connection' as well as an emotional articulacy between the sisters, (Roberts 2008: 212). For the 1991 production, Lesley Sharp noted Angie's 'cunning and slyness' and speculated how Angie might have developed under different circumstances (Roberts 2008: 216–17). In 2011 Olivia Poulet (Angie) was disinclined to heroise Joyce, acknowledged Angie's 'guts' despite her 'learning difficulties' and could appreciate that Angie 'has something of Marlene in her determination to get to London and see her aunt'.[24] For Poulet, both Joyce and Marlene are complicit in Angie's oppression, but Marlene has the economic means to intervene if she so chooses. The education system as well as Marlene and Joyce all fail Angie, Poulet argues:

> When Marlene delivers the line 'She's not going to make it' [*Plays 2* 1990: 120], you feel the audience recoil in shock and disgust. But Joyce has also condemned her. At the end of the play, she describes Angie as 'stupid, lazy and frightened' and predicts that 'her children will say what a wasted life she had' [*Plays 2* 1990: 140]. In many respects Angie is the linchpin of the play, but neither of these adult women is invested in doing anything about her life and neither can overcome their resentment of the other: Angie seems like an object they use to wage war on each other but they consign her to a future without opportunity or hope.[25]

Angie is another of Churchill's failed children, damaged and neglected by those who should protect, not ill but potentially both violent and vulnerable to violence (*Plays 2* 1990: 98–99). In 2011/12, Poulet and Catz were not only unsentimental about Joyce and her

Figure 5.2 Suranne Jones and Olivia Poulet in *Top Girls*, Trafalgar Studios, London © John Haynes

decision to raise Angie, they saw Joyce's passivity as politically complicit with an ideology she claims to oppose. This suggests that critiques such as Kritzer's, which argue that *Top Girls* presents a dialectic based on a gender-based division of labour that opposes an ethic of caring with an ethic of competition, may be too simplistic (Kritzer 1991). Such critiques assume that the principal carer is always female, have overlooked the question of what Joyce's 'caring' amounts to, and presumed that for a woman to choose family over career is inherently virtuous. Such analyses also assume that domestic politics are apolitical – a myth Churchill has spent her entire life endeavouring to explode. Kritzer, like many others, focuses only on Marlene's rejection of Angie that, she argues, 'makes the emphatic point that acquisition of power by a woman who has no concern for the powerless does not constitute a feminist victory' (Kritzer 1991: 141–42). But what of a woman like Joyce who self-destructively refuses to ask for help or accept it when offered? In the 2011/12 revivals, the feud between the two sisters seemed devastating, irreparable and full of hatred, and not at all like a heated argument between two people who love one another.

MARLENE: Come on, Joyce, what a night. You've got what it takes.
JOYCE: I know I have.
MARLENE: I didn't really mean all that.
JOYCE: I did.
MARLENE: But we're friends anyway.
JOYCE: I don't think so, no.

(*Plays 2* 1990: 141)

At the end, Marlene is denied a place domestically, but it is a locus and identity she fled long ago. Marlene is effectively ejected, although she is the one who originally ran away and she seems to see no irony in trying to appeal to the very person she exploited in the first place. In the twenty-first century, the gulf between the sisters has become unbridgeable, and Caroline Catz found the ending particularly devastating: 'Every night I felt shaken by the horror of that contradiction and it left audiences reeling.'[26]

It is poignant that performers in 2011/12 were more alert to the destruction women can wreak on one other, had far less investment in imagining a positive bond between Marlene and Joyce, and condemned Joyce as much as and sometimes more than Marlene. It suggests that there is more willingness to consider the issue of women's complicity in the 'institution of motherhood', a thesis for which Adrienne Rich was denounced in 1976 and which was doubtless familiar to Churchill (Rich 1976). It is further proof that Thatcher's individualist philosophy has taken root and that beliefs in feminist collectivism have lost ground. At the same time, there is a more nuanced understanding of Angie's predicament and a much deeper sense of frustration about her wasted potential. These reactions mirror fierce debates about schooling in Britain and the fact that human rights issues in relation to children have gained greater visibility in the last three decades. In turn, although contraception has allowed women to control when they have children, inflexible and financially disadvantageous employment infrastructures still pose serious impediments to women reaching the top of their profession.[27] During the London run, Olivia Poulet reported:

> The writing is extraordinary. Caryl really does understand how women speak to each other – and in my experience so many playwrights still write stilted and rather unbelievable dialogue for their female characters. The visceral quality of the writing is a real gift to actors and we have found we can powerfully connect with audiences. We're finding that women are coming out of the play quite shell-shocked. They find it staggering that *Top Girls* was written in 1982 and the issues are the same. Work place dilemmas, poor promotion prospects, prejudices and discrimination have not gone away – in fact, some might say it's worse because post-feminism has been destructive and served to obscure issues. Many women of course relate totally to the working woman/mother agonies. You can't 'have it all' and most do have to make sacrifices and compromises and suffer guilt at not being perfect.[28]

Suranne Jones found that audience members' responses in 2011 matched the change in performers' responses. In interview she noted that the polarized 'anti-Marlene, pro-Joyce' audience reactions to the premiere had given way to greater sympathy for Marlene and to a greater understanding of Churchill's project to show how she has become what she has become. Jones is of the view that *Top Girls* hits home more effectively in the twenty-first century and that Churchill was 'ahead of her time' when she wrote it.

> If you ask yourself what has changed for women since the 1980s, I think you have to say that while more women go out to work, corporations still haven't modfied their employment practices and women at the top are scarce. *Top Girls* also remains a hit because it's a play about family and emotional ties and attachments. The theme of strong women in history resonates: we ask what worked then and works now or doesn't

work. Audiences are compelled by the way larger frames of working life, education, opportunity and social welfare are drawn around questions of domestic politics. We all face those issues and the decisions for women are much starker because, despite the rhetoric, equality is low on the political agenda.[29]

The actors' testimonies indicate that Churchill's agenda of employment and educational rights for women has become, if anything, an even more burning issue and that the representation of women's rights on main stages is still all too much of a rarity.

Top Girls: contentious responses

Above I have outlined changing views in relation to Stafford-Clark's production of *Top Girls* in England. It may be Churchill's most celebrated play but its reception history is anything but straightforward. At its premiere, critics were either impressed or bamboozled by the audacious originality of the opening scene, and surprisingly few commented on how startling it must have been to see a large all-female cast.[30] Today *Top Girls* is an important part of the twentieth-century history of British drama, but its exalted status in Britain poses other difficulties. The burdens of representativeness that have been placed upon it are misconceived and have made it hard to separate the play from a set of questionable assumptions. In retrospective British theatre histories of the twentieth century it is common for *Top Girls* to be cited as the only feminist playtext of the 1980s, and all too often it is categorised as representative both of Churchill's career and of women's playwriting in general. The erroneous argument that successful female playwrights were a rare phenomenon before the 1980s, has resulted in some tokenistic historical treatments (Shellard 1999; Eyre and Wright 2000). And critics such as Benedict Nightingale revealed the full extent of their sexism in statements such as: 'After *Top Girls* it was no longer possible to patronise "women dramatists" as some promising but lesser species of creative creature.'[31] Stafford-Clark has explained the confusion in the following terms:

> *Top Girls* gained an importance that was out of proportion to the script on its own terms because both Caryl and the play

Figure 5.3 Lisa Kerr and Olivia Poulet in *Top Girls*, Trafalgar Studios, London © John Haynes

were turned into role models by critics, theorists and pedagogues. I'm not saying it isn't an extraordinary play. In my view it's a triumph of observation over theory – whether feminism or party politics, but I think debates about the play became colonised by generalised commentaries that the 1980s had invented a new sort of female playwright. Women had always been writing plays but subsidised theatre suddenly appreciated that there was a market interest in promoting women's issues.

Few remember that the premiere at the Royal Court got a mixed reception. It was the transfer to New York and its success there which ensured that the production was greeted with unambiguous enthusiasm when it returned to London.[32]

International responses

Different cultures and communities respond distinctly to *Top Girls*, depending on economic pressures, local understandings of parenting and rights for women, and on cultural and/or religious constructions of motherhood versus the working woman. It is a common misconception that women writers betray feminism if they do not represent women positively and Churchill has certainly suffered from this fallacy. In the USA critics were fascinated by the premiere but thought the play backfired inadvertently into anti-feminism because of Churchill's supposedly unsympathetic representations of her female characters. 'Are these feminists too hard on women?' asked critic Walter Kerr, in the *New York Times*, suggesting that Marlene was purely heroic.[33] In 2002, British journalist Julie Burchill denounced *Top Girls* for conveying the message that 'women shouldn't succeed at work because that's "acting like a man"' – an idea that 'appalled' Churchill.[34] Since 1989 and the fall of communism there has been a particular preoccupation with *Top Girls* in Eastern Europe because career choice for women has become more open although views about women in the workplace remain conservative. In fact, directors and educators have many times deployed the play as a vehicle to highlight anti-feminist messages in order to condemn women who both pursue a career and raise children. This has pained Churchill because it formed no part of her agenda. She has voiced her disillusion with productions in other European countries that have represented the characters as exaggeratedly 'neurotic', 'incapable', 'miserable' and 'quarrelsome', and expressed frustration that some theatre-makers have used the play as a vehicle to argue that 'women *shouldn't* go out to work' and turned it into 'a complete travesty of what it was supposed to be' (Roberts 2008: 211). At once the most celebrated feminist play of its time, it is also vulnerable to anti-feminist and hostile post-feminist readings – a depressing indication of how furiously contested the concept of the working mother still is.

One of the most unexpected controversies about *Top Girls* blew up in the state of New South Wales (NSW) in Australia in 1997, when a panel of educationalists and the NSW minister for education declared that the play was unsuitable reading for schoolchildren and recommended its removal from the curriculum. Objections cited were gratuitous violence, offensive sexual references (a scene in which a teenager, Angie, tastes her own menstrual blood), anti-Christian sentiments (the portrayal of anti-family values and life as hopeless) and crude language. For several months *Top Girls* became the subject of heated debate about art, education and censorship in Australia, and students and progressive teachers and arts activists passionately defended it in the press and on the air. *Top Girls* momentarily became a touchstone for an argument for greater openness and for educational and social reform designed to end oppressive paternalist interventions by the state. Underlying those debates was an ugly misogyny. The playwright Nick Enright made a powerful case for children to be allowed the right to 'information and experience which their parents may have forgotten or deny ever having known'.[35] Churchill remained stoically ironic: 'I think teenagers have a much more shocking time in their everyday lives.'[36] The furore only reinforced Churchill's status as an innovative experimenter and productions at Australian universities increased.

Happily, there are other inspiring responses. In China, Churchill is virtually unknown, unlike Pinter, but may yet prove important in terms of feminist resistance to state prejudice and oppression. Female Chinese playwrights struggle to acquire visibility and women's issues are still subject to crushing censorship. Jiyang Qian, a Chinese scholar, has translated *Top Girls*, and she see its Chinese publication and production as an important means of foregrounding debates about women's rights in China.[37]

As Susan Faludi has argued in *Backlash* (1991), constructions of feminism have become alarmingly debased, despite continuing inequality and discrimination, and – in some cultures – the violent repression and censorship of women. It is not surprising that *Top Girls* has been and remains so contentious. The fact that it is repeatedly performed is a testament to the power of the controversies about the politics of reproduction and childrearing that it generates. The dilemma of the work/life balance for contemporary women is anything but solved and, as Michel Billington said of the 2011 revival, *Top Girls* reminds us that 'isolated female success still obscures the plight of the majority'.[38] Female executives who dare to suggest that women are conditioned to hold themselves back at the workplace, and that the revolution has stalled, can find themselves vilified by other women. As I write, Sheryl Sandberg, *Forbes*' fifth most powerful female in the world and chief operating officer at Facebook, is being attacked for writing the bestseller *Lean In: Women, Work and the Will to Lead*, which suggests that women need to rise to the challenges of negotiating the interplay between the demands of work and motherhood and address not just the external but also the internal obstacles to their advancement. The internal obstacles are 'often dismissed and underplayed', argues Sandberg, 'female leaders are key to the solution' and women can 'reignite the revolution by internalising the revolution' (Sandberg 2013: 9, 11). In parallel with Churchill's private life, Sandberg stresses the importance of equality in domestic politics, and reminds us that 'the promise of equality is not the same as real equality' (Sandberg 2013: 7). Indeed, for many millions of women even the battle for an education and the right to a profession has not yet been won.[39]

Notes

1 Benedict Nightingale, *The Times*, 18 August 2013.
2 Dominic Sandford, 'The Age of Superwoman: Margaret Thatcher and the 1980s' in programme to Out of Joint's production of *Top Girls*, Trafalgar Studios, London, 2011.
3 See Andy McSmith, *No Such Thing as Society: A History of Britain in the 1980s* (London: Constable, 2010).
4 See Andrew Gamble, *The Free Economy and the Strong State* (Durham: Duke University Press, 1988).
5 Dominic Sandford, *Top Girls* theatre programme, 2011.
6 Meaning 'young urban professionals', a phrase generally attributed to Jacob Epstein.
7 Public interview of Max Stafford-Clark by Mary Luckhurst, Dixon Theatre, University of York, 8 December 2004.
8 Frank Rich, *New York Times*, 29 December 1982.
9 Author's interview with Max Stafford-Clark, 8 December 2004.
10 Author's interview with Max Stafford-Clark, 8 December 2004.
11 When Sarah Kane was attacked for *Blasted*, Churchill publicly defended Kane's mixture of realism and the surreal as an attempt 'to show connections between local, domestic violence and the atrocities of war'. See Caryl Churchill, *The Guardian*, 23 January 1995.

12 Frank Rich, *New York Times*, 29 December 1982.
13 Author's interview with Max Stafford-Clark, 8 December 2004.
14 Pope Joan was the subject of a film by Sonke Wortmann in 2009.
15 See Bill Ashcroft, Garth Griffiths and Helen Tiffin, *The Empire Writes Back* (London: Routledge, 1989) and Ania Loomba, *Colonialism/Postcolonialism* (London: Routledge, 2005).
16 Author's interview with Olivia Poulet, 23 August 2011.
17 Author's interview with Suranne Jones, 23 August 2011.
18 Author's interview with Olivia Poulet, 23 August 2011.
19 Interview with Caroline Catz by Katherine MacAlistair, *Oxford Mail*, 19 January 2012.
20 Author's public platform interview with Caroline Catz, University of York, 29 February 2012.
21 Author's interview with Caroline Catz, 29 February 2012.
22 Records at the Office of National Statistics for England and Wales demonstrate that births for mothers aged 40 or over have trebled from 9,717 in 1990 to 27,731 in 2010. See also Casilda Grigg, 'Older Mothers: Late Bloomers', *Daily Telegraph*, 11 March 2013.
23 'Lone mothers' are, however, recognised sociologically. See Jonathan Bradshaw et al, *Absent Fathers?* (London: Routledge, 1999).
24 Author's interview with Olivia Poulet, 23 August 2011.
25 Author's interview with Olivia Poulet, 23 August 2011.
26 Author's interview with Caroline Catz, 29 February 2012.
27 Some of that opposition comes from women, see 'Childless Women Resent Female Colleagues Wanting Flexible Working Hours', www.news.com.au/lifestyle/ parenting/childlesswomen.html (accessed 11 March 2013).
28 Author's interview with Olivia Poulet, 23 August 2011.
29 Author's interview with Suranne Jones, 23 August 2011; and Caroline Catz, *Oxford Mail*, 19 January 2012.
30 *London Theatre Record*, vol. II, 26 August–8 September 1982.
31 Benedict Nightingale, *The Times*, 16 April 1991.
32 Author's interview with Max Stafford-Clark, 8 December 2004.
33 Walter Kerr, *New York Times*, 23 January 1983.
34 Caryl Churchill, *The Guardian*, 23 February 2002.
35 Nick Enright, 'What Should Our Children Read?' *The Sydney Papers* 1997, 113.
36 Caryl Churchill, *Australian Daily Telegraph*, 12 March 1997.
37 Jiyang Qian, 'Caryl Churchill in China', Caryl Churchill Symposium, University of Lincoln, 16 April 2010.
38 Michael Billington, *The Guardian*, 4 July 2011.
39 Unesco report that 26 per cent of girls in Pakistan are illiterate and that poverty means many work as domestic help, see www.unesco.org/ education/efa/knowledgesharing/grassroots stories/pakistan (accessed 11 March 2013). The battle for the right for girls to be educated in Pakistan is ongoing, see www.unicefusa.org/news-from-the-field/feeding-girls-hunger.html (accessed 11 March 2013).

Part IV

Revolution and Cross-Artform Experiments, 1990–2000

6   Key Production: *Mad Forest*

The process of researching, writing and experiencing performances of *Mad Forest* in England and in Romania in 1990 was perhaps the most politically and artistically self-confrontational venture that Churchill has undertaken. The play is an inspired endeavour to offer glimpses of life in Romania before, during and after the 1989 revolution. Fuelled by the rapid collapse of communist government in Poland, Hungary, Czechoslovakia, Bulgaria and East Germany, and by the breaching of the Berlin Wall in November 1989, which had been a symbol of the separation between the communist East and the capitalist West (Stokes 1993; Garton Ash 2000; Engel 2009), Romanians began mass demonstrations in Timisoara in mid-December. Riots had begun with the announcement of the eviction of Laszlo Toekes, a Hungarian Protestant priest in Timisoara, a town with a large Hungarian minority population (Rady 1992: 91–98). Swollen by students from two universities in Timisoara, the protest spread to Bucharest, and reprisals by the Securitate, the secret police, were fierce but the Romanian army sided with the people and fought the last remaining die-hards. The uprising led to the notorious dictator, Nicolae Ceausescu, and his wife, Elena, making a dramatic helicopter escape from the rooftop of the Central Committee Building only to be executed by firing squad two days later on 25 December 1989 (Behr 1991). More people were killed after the deaths of the Ceausescus than during the week-long uprising as forces loyal to Ceausescu tried to cling on to power. For that week the world was mesmerised by the violent television images emerging from Romania, which had hitherto been closed off to the West. The total number of victims shot to death in December 1989 was estimated to be 1,200.[1]

'Television made the revolution; television is the revolution,' Aurel Munteanu, the first director of the Free Romanian Television, was later to declare, acknowledging the role of the media in the revolution and the fact that Romanians had watched its progress on foreign news channels (Rady 1992: 99). Ceausescu's communist dictatorship lasted from 1965 to 1989 and, although Romania 'possessed more aspects of totalitarian dictatorship than any other of the east-European party-states', comparatively little has been written on his brutal tenure (Gallagher 1995: 73; Behr 1991; Pacepa 1988). Churchill's drama is an extraordinary and unique attempt to reflect on the end of a totalitarian regime and the post-Wall transition to a new political future – this liminal present has been referred to by Zaborowska as 'Era X' and is yet to be named by political theorists.[2]

After the revolution the gap between Ceausescu's propaganda and his luxurious lifestyle started to emerge; as one Balkan expert phrased it, 'the extravagance of this dictatorship was without precedent in European communist history' (Glenny 2012: 602). Romanians were stunned: they had suffered severe privations, especially of electricity and gas, had been denied freedom of speech and movement, kept under continual surveillance, suffered extensive food rationing and material poverty that meant days of queueing (often in vain), and lived in terror of the Securitate's torture and infiltration tactics (Deletant 1995). By 1989 the Securitate employed 24,000 officers but its groundlings were the hundreds of thousands of informers who reported on the activities of citizens at every level of society.[3] In historian Misha Glenny's words:

> The prisons, psychiatric units and torture sessions represented the sharp end of the Securitate, but made up only a small part of its activity. For most people, the terror consisted in the certainty that one of your close friends or family was informing on you, contributing to the detailed files that the Securitate opened on every citizen. One Romanian writer reflected: 'In the socialist world, people and things exist only in personal files. The owner of these files is the owner of all existence.'
>
> (Glenny 2012: 604)[4]

Ceausescu's dictatorship invaded every aspect of life: his legislation decreed that a woman's body belonged to the state and every fertile female endured a gynaecological examination each month to verify or disprove conception since a failure to produce a child was a failure of state duty (Glenny 2012: 604). Entire historic quarters of Bucharest and other cities were bulldozed, and agricultural workers forcibly removed to collective farms in the name of 'systematisation' (Glenny 2012: 608). Hungarian, Jewish and Roma populations were programmatically persecuted and many were tortured to death. From the Western media's viewpoint, one of the most devastating legacies of Ceausescu's regime, aside from the resurgence of ethnic conflict, were the vast numbers of orphaned and displaced children, many of them dysfunctional from years of shocking emotional and physical neglect in hidden camp orphanages.[5] Churchill's play comes at these living nightmares obliquely, the form in itself suggestive of double lives, hidden torments, enforced silences and nagging uncertainties.

Directed by Mark Wing-Davey, *Mad Forest* was first performed by final-year acting students on 25 June 1990 at the Embassy Studio, Central School of Speech and Drama (CSSD) in London, then at the National Theatre of Romania in Bucharest in September, the production finally transferring to the Royal Court from 12–27 October 1990. In November and December 1991, Wing-Davey directed a professional production at the New York Theater Workshop with a cast that included Liev Schreiber and Calista Flockhart; he went on to direct it at the Berkeley Rep in November 1992 and at Pittsburgh in 1993. Since its premiere, *Mad Forest* has become a significant play for students on drama programmes at universities and conservatoires in Europe, America, Asia and Australia. As Claire Armitstead has argued, it is especially appropriate for students to enact *Mad Forest* because the university quarter in Bucharest was one of the prime sites of the uprising, and thousands of students gave their voice, and many their lives, to the revolution.[6] Indeed, the play's large cast, with its requirement for multiple role-playing, and its epic scope are precisely what make it perfect for ambitious students to produce and economically difficult for professional companies to accommodate. Churchill, as a mother, was no doubt very conscious of the sacrifice made by so many young people, and Martyn Rady does not hesitate to mark their bravery in helping to bring about the end of an horrific era:

Throughout the period of confused fighting and gunfire, crowds remained on the streets, sheltering behind tanks and in doorways and bringing food to the soldiers. The vast majority of these consisted of young people aged between 16 and 25. The extraordinary courage they displayed in this part of the conflict may be explained in terms of a genuine desire to help the army and a natural wish to be present in the making of history. Surviving accounts suggest, however, that the willingness of young people to participate in this phase of the struggle assumed early on the dimension of a profoundly moral act. As Ana Blandiana was later to put it, 'the innocent and tempestuous blood' shed on the streets of Bucharest had in some mysterious way purified 'the stale and dirty waters' thrown up 'from the desperate bank' of Romania's recent history.

(Rady 1992: 111)[7]

The idea of making a play about the Romanian revolution first occurred to Wing-Davey as he absorbed events from the news in December 1989. At the time he was artistic director at CSSD and realised that those dying were the same age as his students. He knew Churchill from their time together at Joint Stock and rang her with an invitation to do a workshop in Romania.

As a socialist who'd followed the collapse of communism in other countries, she felt it was important to go and see what was happening for herself. Caryl and I went for three days in March 1990 – out there we asked ourselves what we knew and didn't know about the revolution and we formulated a whole set of questions about what life was like before the revolution. We visited staff and students at the Caragiale Institute of Theatre and Film Arts in Bucharest and ran improvisation workshops with them. I set up an exchange project between the CSSD and the Caragiale Institute and, after a short break, Caryl and I went back again in April for a week and took with us 11 acting students, a lighting designer and a set designer. The Romanian and British students worked together and we did a whole set of acting exercises using Joint Stock methods.[8]

Wing-Davey has described the acting exercises as 'a springboard for the writer's imagination', and confirmed that many scenes from the play evolved from improvisation exercises and directed scenarios.[9]

Churchill and Wing-Davey also made a list of possible occupations for characters, having discussed their mutual desire to try and represent the revolution from the perspectives of ordinary people, whether they had participated or hidden inside their homes. The Romanian students told their stories, but both sets of students also did fieldwork in the manner of Joint Stock character studies (a method in which the CSSD students were particularly accomplished) – conducting interviews about the revolution with members of the general public and recording their words carefully, complete with pauses and personality tics, and then mimicking the interviewee back in the theatre studio with as much linguistic and physical accuracy as possible. Romanian students directed British students in given scenarios and vice versa.[10] While most of the ideas for the play came from the workshop in Romania, and Churchill amassed many ideas for scenes, she also researched extensively and watched and listened to a great deal of news footage. One of the more developed characters in *Mad Forest*, Lucia, came from a serendipitous encounter in New York during which Churchill heard the story of a Romanian woman who had left her country to marry an American, thereby greatly endangering her family, only to discover that things in the USA were not as perfect as she had imagined.[11]

Churchill's first-hand experiences in a newly liberated Romania had a profound impact on both the content and form of *Mad Forest*. According to Wing-Davey, everyone in the British party was overwhelmed by feelings of disorientation and incomprehension.[12] One aspect of the workshops in Romania, therefore, focused on the expression of the culture shock experienced by the British visitors. Every day Wing-Davey asked the British acting students to improvise two minutes of Romanian life that they had witnessed. Common motifs emerged and heavily informed the play. These included the challenge of finding simple foodstuffs, and the constant rebuttal of expectations and the difficulty of everyday living, such as the non- or erratic functionality of electrical machinery, especially phones, light sources and elevators. The Britons also found that they misread and misunderstood situations they found themselves in or Romanians with whom they conversed. They observed the Romanian habituation to queuing for basic items for extremely long hours, and found it hard to grasp the paranoia about the change in regime. The intense suspicion surrounding the circumstances of

Ceausescu's death, whether he was really dead or not, and conspiracy theories as to whether there had been a revolution or simply
a putsch, struck all the British participants, Churchill herself later
commenting that Romanian society demonstrated 'a whole spectrum of paranoia at one end, stretching through to a very reason-
able suspicion at the other'.[13] In response to the political paranoia
they encountered, Wing-Davey invented a series of exercises that he
called 'truth and lies': the Romanian and British students presented
improvisations to each other and had to guess who was telling the
truth and who was lying.[14] Under Ceausescu Romanians always
feared that a family or friend might have turned informer and
appearances could never be believed. In his novel, *Refuges* (1984),
Augustin Buzura captured something of the incapacitating terror
and alienation experienced by most Romanians:

> I am afraid of running away, but also of staying, of roaring, but
> also of keeping silent, of living, but of dying too [...] I'm afraid
> of lying, but am unable to tell the truth. I'm afraid of night, of
> light, of people ... I fear everything! I'd stay here if I knew
> nobody would come ... I'd leave if nobody looked for me, if they
> didn't recognise me, if I didn't have to answer questions.[15]

Much of *Mad Forest* explores the extreme fear and states of paranoia that Buzura describes. It was no surprise to Wing-Davey that
the Romanian students proved much more adept at playing sincerity
and at demonstrating ingenious, covert strategies of communicating.[16] In fact the difficulties or impossibilities of communication,
both in times of dictatorship and afterwards, and in particular the
problems experienced by the British participants of trying to
negotiate a language barrier, as well as immersion in a totally
unfamiliar culture, very much came to inform Churchill's dramaturgical ideas for *Mad Forest*. In turn, the experience of the workshop in Romania became fundamental, in Wing-Davey's view, to
the quality of the acting in performance and he insisted on parallel
preparation for actors in his American productions, and required
them to conduct interviews with Romanians in their respective
environs.[17] Wing-Davey's process of making *Mad Forest* therefore
became as significant as his productions since it directly introduced
particular American actors to Joint Stock methods.

The London premiere: geographies of form and language

In the published playtext of *Mad Forest*, Churchill includes an epigraph to explain its title:

> On the plain where Bucharest now stands there used to be 'a large forest crossed by muddy streams ... It could only be crossed on foot and was impenetrable for the foreigner who did not know the paths ... The horsemen of the steppe were compelled to go round it, and this difficulty, which irked them so, is shown by the name ... Teleorman – Mad Forest.'
>
> (Plays 3 1998: 103)

The title alludes to the impossibility of foreign visitors navigating their way through 'impenetrable' paths to Bucharest, and Churchill's play mirrors both those thwarted journeys to the centre of the city, and her own sense that she managed to catch only glimpses of the lives and issues she was attempting to capture. The subtitle is specifically 'A Play from Romania', not '*about* Romania' and Wing-Davey is clear that:

> The key thing about *Mad Forest* is that it's not a play about Romania, it's a play about what it's like to watch a play about Romania. Not-knowing, not understanding were themselves very important ideas in its making. The play tries to generate a sense of cultural dislocation in the audience.[18]

It is precisely this cultural dislocation that is inscribed into the play through the multiple role-play of the 11 actors (who play more than 37 parts), through its linguistic self-referentiality, and its collapsing together of radically different theatrical and performative styles.

The form of *Mad Forest* appears to be a conventional three-act play: Act I 'Lucia's Wedding'; Act II 'December'; Act III 'Florina's Wedding'. In fact, in Acts I and III, actors play multiple roles in snapshot scenes that momentarily steal glances at the situation of two families, the Vladus, who are artisans, and the more educated Antonescus. Act I is set before the revolution under Ceausescu and ends with Lucia's marriage to an American, the symbol of her 'escape' to the West. Act III is located post-revolution and ends with Florina's marriage to Radu, not previously sanctioned by Radu's family for political reasons (namely, her sister Lucia's 'unpatriotic' love-match). The American Dream having proved empty, Lucia has returned to Romania, and in a mercenary manoeuvre, tries to revivify a relationship with Ianos, a Hungarian. Florina's wedding ends in a cacophonous bacchanalia of dancing, abusive shouting matches and physical violence. The sudden implosion of a traditionally happy day into a volley of base nationalist and ethnic abuse has a hauntingly apocalyptic edge. Act II fractures the play into two discernible parts: there are no figures in it who appear elsewhere in the play, and it contains a collection of direct-address speeches about what various individuals did when the revolution broke out and how it made them feel. While it bridges the play in terms of narrative and historical chronology, Act II is otherwise a radical disjuncture and a stark alienation device, interrupting fiction with stylised verbatim accounts from Romanians interviewed by Churchill and the cast.[19] Wing-Davey deployed a documentary style that eschewed acting behind a fourth wall, and performers stood in front of the safety curtain as if for a group photograph. The form of Act II was therefore made to stand in ironic relation to its content: stasis and restraint replaced movement and actors resisted heightened vocalisation:

> When the revolution arrives it does so through the reminiscences of a stageful of citizens who recount, in deadpan tones, their own chronology of events according to where and how they were standing at the time: a glamorous girl student weeps for shame at being locked away from the action by her father; a house-painter tells of the siege on the television station; a flower-seller regrets the marriage and premature motherhood that forces her to keep her head down.[20]

Critics disagreed about the device itself, but were arrested by the sudden formal explosion of the play. Irving Wardle noted that the ingenious effect of this 'chorus of revolutionary eye-witnesses' was to make 'Churchill's voice dissolve into the anonymity of the Living Newspaper'.[21] Jeremy Kingston, like many, felt somewhat spooked:

> They stare out at us, unaware of each other, speaking with slight Romanian accents [...] the device gives a startlingly vivid

sense of real events being recalled in the immediate aftermath. The style is *théâtre verité*, rich in the absurd or homely details people do remember at such times, and this section is the most wholly satisfying of the three acts.[22]

In a production note to *Mad Forest*, Churchill describes the dramaturgy of the play as going 'from the difficulty of saying anything to everyone talking' (*Plays 3* 1998: 104). 'Don't be afraid of long silences,' Churchill advises; short, silent scenes 'need to be given their weight'; 'the queue scenes and the execution scene should have as many people as are available'; and the temptation to add dialogue or speak during scenes where time is stretched – perhaps to an excruciating degree for actor and audience – should be resisted (*Plays 3* 1998: 104). The premiere was noted for its bold use of silence and attention to small details of radical action, such as the worker, Radu, who whispers 'Down with Ceausescu' while queueing for food, the only line of the scene (*Plays 3* 1998: 111); and the tender moment when Ianos places his hand over Lucia's watch as they steal time together in a world where they have virtually no control over their own lives (*Plays 3* 1998: 120). John Gross's complaint that 'sometimes the portrayal of tedium is all too realistic' was a sign only of the cast's successful refusal to make compromises for London audiences.[23] If the revolution brought freedom of speech and the right to voice an independent opinion without fear, then Churchill's play shows a sonic landscape that moves from uneasy silences, snatched, illicit moments of freedom of expression where figures reveal their opposition to the regime, to a Romanian tower of Babel that is far from utopian. The physical plotting of the play mirrors linguistic patterns, moving from scenes of stasis to wild bursts of activity in Act III, including the madcap mock execution of the Ceausescus in scene 3 and the frenzied final scene that zanily juxtaposes a classic silent slapstick routine with the volcanic eruption of dancing and intercutting voices (*Plays 3* 1998: 177–81).

Churchill's own attempts to learn Romanian provided the inspiration for the scene headings, which are cited first in Romanian and then in English, and styled in the manner of a tourist phrasebook: for example, '*Cumparam carne.* We are buying meat' and '*Ascultati?* Are you listening?' headings were read out by members of the company suggesting that ideas of cultural and linguistic translation were under particular scrutiny.[24] Critic Irving Wardle gave an eloquent description of how he experienced the effect of Churchill's dramaturgy:

> It is written from the viewpoint of an outsider, picking up scraps of evidence like beach pebbles, and gradually assembling them into a pattern which, however incomplete, is made of solid materials. The spectator moves likewise from the known to the unknown.[25]

It is fitting that the play ends with a chaotic storm of Romanian phrases, freedom of expression now won (even if everything else seems uncertain), forcing a Western audience into linguistic exile, the progressive grammatical complication of the Brechtian scene headings matching the grammar of the play structure. For Eastern European critics such as Ludmilla Kostova, Churchill's decision to embed herself into the play demonstrates an ethical conscience as she attempts 'an intercultural dialogue in which the dramatist is a participant rather than an omniscient mentor contemplating the exchange from the outside' (Kostova 2000: 90). For Kostova, Churchill's refusal of a linear grand narrative, her juxtaposition of the real and the surreal, the dead with the living, of the imaginary with eye-witness accounts, are all important and honest inscriptions of the confusion of the political moment and of the foreign observer. Bloom points out that Churchill deploys a 'prismatic technique', that her form creates the theatrical equivalent to the 'jump-cut' or the 'subjective camera' in film (Bloom 1990: 64). Other Western playwrights who chose social-realist strategies to depict post-Wall East European chaos were, argues Kostova, presenting a totalising reduction[26]: what makes *Mad Forest* distinctive, she states, is Churchill's 'distrust of the mass media and of the simplistic versions of East European reality they were instrumental in producing' (Kostova 2000: 89).

The 16 fragmentary scenes in Act I all explore the complexities of lives policed by excessive state controls, and the impossibility of communicating anything meaningful without resorting to covert or non-verbal exchanges, deploying coded language, or retreat into the self. In scene 1, all dialogue is obscured by a loud radio designed to foil bugging devices, but we understand from the family's varying reactions to Lucia's gifts of eggs and American cigarettes, that her fraternisation with her American boyfriend is bringing her family to the attention of the Securitate and causing hardship. In scene 5, Radu's one whispered line – 'Down with Ceausescu' – becomes a dangerous protest as shoppers pretend they have not heard and shuffle away from him. In scene 7, Lucia risks her life in arranging an illegal abortion with a doctor who pretends to admonish her but is simultaneously pocketing her bribe. In scene 8, men tell each other cryptic jokes that encode sidelong criticism of the regime. Significantly, the longest monologues are an official panegyric of Ceausescu delivered by a schoolteacher and an interrogation by a member of the Securitate, who is forcing Lucia's father to inform on her. State-sanctioned rhetoric prevails and, like the ceremonial music that acts as a prologue to the play, it acts as a lethal weapon, brainwashing the gullible or ensnaring and terrorising dissenters. Revealingly, the most emotionally invested exchanges occur only in the realms of the imagination: between Flavia and her dead grandmother, and between a priest and an angel called Michael. The priest voices the dilemma of speaking out, and its cost – both spiritual and mortal:

> Someone says something, you say something back, you're called to a police station, that happened to my brother. So it's not safe to go out to people and when you can't go out sometimes you find you can't go in, I'm afraid to go inside myself, perhaps there's nothing there, I just keep still. But I can talk to you, no one's ever known an angel work for the Securitate.
>
> (*Plays 3* 1998: 115)

The priest's desperate need for absolution is more than suspect. Romania's notoriously fascistic Iron Guard was founded by Corneliu Codreanu in 1930 from an existing order known as the Legion of the Archangel Michael, and its members were legendary for their sadistic, anti-Semitic violence, which they coupled with a fanaticism for the Orthodox Church.[27] Their 'death commandos' became especially celebrated after the slaughter of Nicolae Stelescu, whose body they hacked into pieces with an axe and danced around before celebrating with kisses, prayers and tears of joy (Glenny 2012: 448–55). Churchill's surreal exchange between angel and priest is freighted with a dark history: it is the

Figure 6.1 Sophie Larsmon and Alan Stewart in *Mad Forest*, York Theatre Royal © Nikolaus Morris

collapse of personal and collective responsibility, a politics of hypocrisy and denial:

ANGEL: I try to keep clear of the political side. You should do the same.
         Pause.
PRIEST: I don't trust you any more.
ANGEL: That's a pity. Who else can you trust?
         Pause.

WOULD YOU RATHER FEEL ASHAMED?
> *Pause.*
OR ARE YOU GOING TO TAKE SOME KIND OF ACTION, SURELY NOT?
> *Silence.*
PRIEST: Comfort me.

(Plays 3 1998: 116)

The priest's descent into terrorised silence, the opposite of protest, is all too clear. Behind it stands the uncomfortable truth that the Romanian Church was culpably quiescent during Ceausescu's dictatorship, and did not lead organised religious resistance, unlike Churches in neighbouring communist countries. Nothing is what it seems in many of Churchill's scenes: silences are cavernous and might be assenting, dissenting, at odds with actions and words; and they edge towards the treacherous, or even the murderous. Even apparently straightforward cameo scenes become complex, layered cryptograms, which allude to historical and political grand narratives, as well as to the pain and suffering of ordinary individuals.

Another surreal encounter, between a dog and a vampire, marks the beginning of Act III. It is a clear alienation device and stands in contrast to the unforced truthfulness of the verbatim delivery in Act II. But to dress the vampire as a vampire is to miss the point as Churchill indicates in her production note (*Plays 3* 1998: 104). The scene title 'Cîinelui e foame. The dog is hungry,' explains the situation with Brechtian formality, but unlike Brecht the ensuing scene is set in ironic counterpoint to its descriptor – the dog is more hungry for subservience than it is for food and, fatally, invites the vampire to become its master. Indifferent to its fate, the dog is quite willing to submit to the life of a vampire dog, and the scene ends with their new alliance as the vampire '*puts his mouth to the dog's neck*' (*Plays 3* 1998: 139). Packs of wild dogs were common on Romanian streets as Wing-Davey has pointed out,[28] and the deeply-embedded folklore about vampires and Transylvania is well-known. But the vampire is also a manifest allusion to Ceausescu himself, since he had overseen the rewriting of Romanian history, placing himself at its centre by restoring the reputation of Vlad the Impaler and rehabilitating Dracula as his direct precursor with the aim of providing a historical precedent for political tyranny. Indeed, Ceausescu's revisionism was so thorough that a whole floor of the National Museum in Bucharest had been given over to extolling his achievements (Rady 1992: 46). What we have in this scene is something similar to Beckett's interrogation of master/slave narratives through the creation of Pozzo and Lucky in *Waiting for Godot*. Post-revolution, the vampire is directly implicated in the shedding of blood, but the dog, now free, is disoriented and starving, suffering a self-destructive longing for authority. The dog, habituated to subjugation, simply takes the next opportunity to become a servant – to a master who only promises more killing:

VAMPIRE: All that happens is you begin to want blood, you try to put it off, you're bored with killing, but you can't sit quiet, you can't settle to anything, your limbs ache, your head burns, you have to keep moving faster and faster, that eases the pain, seeking. And finding. Ah.

(*Plays 3* 1998: 139)

A symbolic scene of self-immolation and a reminder that material deprivation and poverty provide a dangerous engine to the political machinery of state, it is significant that this encounter leads into an Act III that teems with doubts, paranoia, conspiracy theories and terror about whether the change in regime will be lasting and meaningful. The dog also acts as a symbol of the vexed question of why opposition to Ceausescu was so weak: Glenny has highlighted the high numbers of first generation immigrants, the majority peasant population, the long lineage of ruling cliques, and the terrifying efficacy of the Securitate; Falk has discussed the dilemmas of dissidence (Glenny 2012: 606; Falk 2003).[29] The fact that the vampire's words are repeated, indeed are the last words to resound clearly from the cacophony of voices at the end of the play, is a dark and doom-laden note: in Churchill's view, the Romanian past and present place heavy burdens on the future and suggest repeated cycles of violence.

The oblique interrogations at the heart of *Mad Forest* place many demands on its audiences but the confounding of expectation is a critical part of the play's purpose and was an integral part of the design concept. It is a piece that makes explicit the problem of writing about 'the ethnography of the Other' (Mitchell 1993: 506), and which continually problematises the relationship between the seen and unseen. Wing-Davey has said that he and Churchill wanted the experience of watching the play to reflect some of their experience of being in Romania: 'the long silences, the not-knowing, and the waiting [in queues] were attempts to capture some of the atmosphere and the tedium.'[30] His direction further enhanced the audience's disorientation through frequently refusing a single central focus in a scene; instead he included dispersed details of action, unexplained action and inaudible conversation, intentionally creating the sense that more was going on than could be perceived, and that the main narrative focus might be only one side of the story.[31] The set was a bleak, half-finished construction of apartments in grey, graffitied concrete. The audience sat on uncomfortable, breezeblock concrete, which mirrored designer Antony McDonald's breezeblock walls of the set, a reminder of the worst aspects of brutalistic communist architecture. Bright light snapped on at the end of each scene, as if to immortalise the image, perhaps suggest a surveillance camera, or act as a reminder of the interrogation room's relentless glare. The blackout at the end of the play, peppered with rapid gunfire, was sudden and unexpected, redolent of an invisible and malevolent authority about to reinstate itself with dreadful effect.

The National Theatre of Romania

Churchill's trip to Bucharest in July 1990 to see *Mad Forest* premiere in Romania was emotional. Her play underwent the ultimate test in front of audiences who shared a history that Churchill did not share and were now disoriented by a longed-for but bewildering present. Churchill took the unusual step of publishing extracts of her diary in *The Guardian* in order to convey the strange privilege of presenting a fiction of the revolution to those who had lived through it only nine months earlier. She noted that there were fewer soldiers and no tanks on the streets as there had been during her trips in March and April, and that the end of the Ceausescu era felt more persuasively in the past.[32] But Wing-Davey was aware of very fragile sensibilities around him. The distrust of new-found freedoms had been dramatically demonstrated during rehearsals when staff entering the space were panicked by the sound of pre-revolutionary music and feared that the country had slipped back into dictatorship.[33] Their nervousness was doubly understandable: the new leader, Ion Iliescu, had just alarmed many Romanians by inviting the miners to put down the freedom movement demonstrating on the streets of Bucharest. Wing-Davey took the decision to transmit live radio bulletins during the stand-off as an epilogue to the play each night and to act as a reminder of the need to continue the struggle for peace and stability.[34] To a people who had known the worst consequences for taking a stand against the government, Wing-Davey's decision was terrifying.

Churchill's anxiousness at the time is palpable from her diary. She was particularly alert to the introduction of objects and clothes to the production that rent the stage fiction with their resonances of the historical reality outside the theatre building.

Sunday
The company is here already and has assembled a new set – old metal, real shrine. Real soldiers' uniforms borrowed from the army. The space is three sides like the Embassy Studio (where we've been playing), 400 seats like the Royal Court (where we go next).[35]

The real shrine had a transgressive resonance in signifying the new freedom of expression, and prompted reflection on Toekes, whose eviction had sparked the origin of the revolution. It also transformed the stage into a site of memorialisation, bringing the reality of numerous deaths and untold suffering before, during and after the revolution directly into the playing area. It ensured that actors performed in a site marked out for a sacred ritual of memory, which could at no time be forgotten, the actual soldiers' uniforms becoming at once signifiers of a history of terror, murder, betrayal, hopelessness and yet victory. Actors wondered whether the soldier who had owned their 'costume', a second skin for them during the run, had tortured or maimed or killed anyone; and asked themselves which side the soldier had been on and whether they were a hero or a villain, and indeed, whether they had survived the revolution or not.[36] In their decisions to incorporate these elements into the design, the cast appear to have wanted to dilute the purely metaphorical world of theatre, and to show up the contrivance of art even more than Churchill's already self-reflexive structure signalled. Creative fictions had been lethal under Ceausescu – artists had been censored, tortured and executed. Faced with audiences who were in the process of consciously scripting their lives anew, it was as though the cast felt that their own project must embed objects that could create an exchange that was more visceral and stood for something more than the purely representational.

Churchill's description of the first night is terse, and gives a sense of an intense, edgy and emotionally tumultuous evening:

> Monday
> We're nervous. What will Romanians feel about the play? Full house, aisles full of people. Laughter of recognition; silence very thick; some people cry. A little group of middle-aged men leaves without clapping. Someone says there were many *nomenclatura* in the central section of the audience because it was the first night. Most people seemed moved and shocked. 'This is better than any western aid we have had.' 'This is like a second revolution for us.'
>
> Nothing in the theatre ever means as much to an audience in England. Does that mean nothing means as much to us? Or don't we write about the things that do? Do we know what they are? Or is it that so much is written that there's no thrill in it? Or because theatre in Romania has mattered for years because even censored it was one of the few forms of opposition?[37]

It is interesting that the power and profundity of the occasion move Churchill to ask herself fundamental questions about the state of theatre in England – questions that had appeared three decades earlier in her manifesto. This time she is less confident that she has the answers, more mindful of her own cultural blindness and of the privilege of living in a society where individuals do not generally risk their lives for participating in or attending theatre.[38] She is sharply aware that *Mad Forest* is an active example that artistic censorship in Romania is a thing of the past, but wonders whether it is stretching expectation that it be televised.[39] Characteristically self-effacing, Churchill says nothing of her own feelings, but what makes *Mad Forest* unique is the small part it served in the beginnings of Romania's state of transition and self-examination. Her remaining diary entries are a moving testament to this:

Thursday

It's the first time for 30 years a character in a play has been allowed to say things critical of the president in a theatre – will it be allowed on tv? It's the 21st [September] – nine months from the revolution. Candles in the shrine and new flowers on the cross.

[...]

Saturday

By the memorial in University Square, service for the dead. Three cars pull up sharply: a man lays an official wreath. As he gets into his car, people start beating on it, shouting 'Down with communism.'

Discussion after the last show. Someone says they are ashamed that Romanians haven't written a play about the situation yet. I remind them of a line in the play said to us by a painter: 'I didn't want to paint for a long time then,' and they clap and agree. Afterwards a young woman says: 'But really it is because they want to see which way the wind will blow.' A woman of 80: 'After 25 years of suffering, your nerves are stiff and your heart is a stone.' She thanks us for the play and our love. Afterwards I think we're not that good at writing about our own situation. Maybe if a Romanian company came to London, they could hold us a mirror.[40]

Other domestic and international productions

The proximity and immediacy of the events in *Mad Forest* to European audiences were not givens in the early 1990s in the USA, and Wing-Davey's productions had to take this into account. Far from Europe, and with a news network dominated by other matters, Wing-Davey and his designer Marina Draghici had to ensure that Americans at the New York Theater Workshop understood the context of *Mad Forest* and knew how to orientate themselves. For the London premiere, the invisible presence of the Ceausescus had been communicated through the acting, but the New York and Berkeley Rep productions were performed beneath gigantic head-shots of Nicolae and Elena Ceausescu. Draghici and the lighting designer, Christopher Akerlind, focused on visual referents that they knew would find literary resonances, and transformed the labyr-inthine, metaphorical forest into 'into an ever-changing Chinese box of oppressively angled walls and shadowy cul-de-sacs'.[41] *New York Times* critic Frank Rich saw the set as a significant actor in its own right: sliding and shifting panels revealed myriad locations – the interior of someone's home, a doctor's surgery, a hospital, a shop, a school, glimpses of frescos. For Rich it was inventively, disturbingly reminiscent of the fiction of Kundera and Havel.[42] Wing-Davey was convinced of the importance of the effect of material discomfort for the audience, but concrete blocks were replaced by differently sized chairs, some spectators seated close to the floor and others raised up higher. Higgledy-piggledy chaos reigned over plush uniformity and broke up the spectator's sightline. As Wing-Davey elaborated:

> In Romania chairs in the rehearsal rooms were always random selections, ramshackle, quite different sizes, and there usually weren't enough. I wanted to reproduce that idea and I was also thinking about Howard Barker's wonderful essay in *Arguments for a Theatre* (Barker 1989), where he talks about audiences who watch spectacles on seats behaving as judges and audiences who come into found spaces arriving as participants.[43]

Celebrity members of the cast, however, made it much harder to keep the ensemble cohesive, and actors competed to display their role-swapping talents.[44] While the American critics enjoyed this, to be at its best *Mad Forest* requires a disciplined and generous ensemble spirit from the whole cast. For Wing-Davey: 'The raw material is somehow more important than the individual performer. Yet ironically, from the material you get the best sorts of individual performance.'[45]

For directors of later productions, it is the staging of Act II that seems to need most reflection. Tony Mitchell staged a student production at the University of Technology, Sydney, in 1991 and wrote an engrossing essay on *Mad Forest*. As a director on the other side of the world, he felt that Wing-Davey's desire for the audience to be unsettled had to be taken further:

> Performed in corrected English, without Romanian accents, cut fairly extensively, and played with the students coming into a

darkened auditorium and sitting in the audience one by one, carrying candles, in a simulation of the shrines which were set up in Romania (and throughout Eastern Europe). Slides of the Romanian uprising were projected, accompanied by a sound tape of gunfire and crowds, mixed with Romanian music. These atmospheric additions lent support to what we felt was otherwise a blunt and static documentary scene.

(Mitchell 1993: 511)

Mitchell's visceral production spared the audience little, and as such was entirely in keeping with Churchill's interrogation of individual political responsibility. Accents were familiar and the lines of division between actor and audience were removed – all this brought the action directly to each spectator. The counterpoint between the contemplative stillness of the auditorium lit up by numerous candles, each held by a spokesperson in grief and shock, against the bloodshed and terror in the footage of the actual revolution, had gut-wrenching effect.

Mitchell's point about the stasis of purist documentary technique is interesting. In the immediate aftermath of the revolution, Wing-Davey's stasis was appropriate, respectful, and ensured that the centre of attention was as much on the person who had originally spoken the words as on the actor. In later productions that stasis has come to seem unnecessary and to lack punch. The prevalence of documentary and verbatim forms on world stages in the twenty-first century (Cantrell 2013) also means that directors need to work much harder to create a powerful performance. When I directed *Mad Forest* at the York Theatre Royal in 2006, students and young audiences knew little of the Cold War and nothing of the Romanian revolution. Without movement the performance style was old-fashioned. I used the whole cast on stage but individual speeches became vignettes of simple action, the actors nearest the speaker forming tableaux or making simple gestures and movements to underscore the words. In an otherwise frozen mass of people there were always moments of moving sculpture, perhaps someone falling to the ground, someone stretching out a hand to help, someone being lifted or attempting to hide or peek out, or someone being struck. Behind the actors there was a floor-length gauze and projected on to this at certain points slow motion shots of the actors moving, looking shocked or terrified, and every so often black-and-white photographs and footage from the actual revolution. Gunfire was sporadic with one intense volley when all the actors threw themselves to the floor. Since audiences in 2006 mostly did not know the fate of the Ceausescus, the very end of Act II was marked by the actors assembling themselves into a firing squad and bearing down on the audience, arms outstretched as rifles before a blackout and three thunderous rounds from automatic machine guns. It left the actors and the spectators in shock and the whole act became a *coup de théâtre*.

Director Jonathan Lim's production at the Republic Cultural Centre in Singapore in 2007 exploited the orchestral density of Act II and used song to create moments of crescendo, rallentando and pianissimo. The critic Hong Xinyi was spellbound by the power of the vocal singing and chanting:

> Thirteen performers move in a circle at first, with individuals stepping out to deliver their lines, the rest murmuring snatches of dialogue under their breaths. As gunshots and confusion set in, they scatter like a burst of fireworks, before coming together in a moving tableau of song. The entire thing mesmerises like a taut, fervent dance; the ensemble moves and breathes as one.[46]

Perhaps it is to be expected that a Romanian designer, Dan Potra, who created a set for director Antoinette Blaxland in 1993 for the Australian Theatre for Young People at the Seymour Centre in Sydney, should have felt compelled to build an actual forest. Potra trained at the Nicolae Grigorescu Institute in Bucharest and escaped Romania in 1987, having been asked by the Securitate to inform on and recruit fellow students.[47] Potra's deadwood forest engulfed stage and auditorium because he wanted audiences to 'feel lost in a forest, that a canopy is pressing down on them'.[48] Among the trees, fragments of Romanian flag hung from the ceiling, symbolising lost identities, and the floor was strewn with leaves. The lighting designer, Nigel Levings, placed lights 'wherever he could find a hole in the forest' and found the challenge of working in a cramped set-up artistically 'liberating'.[49] Potra mused on what Churchill's original production must have been like for the people of Bucharest:

I think it was like having a mirror in your house that has been covered up for the twenty-four years of Ceausescu's regime. Suddenly the cover is whipped off and at first you don't recognise yourself. Certainly, on reading the script, I was forced to examine my own sense of identity. When I visited Romania in 1992, I was shocked to discover my contemporaries – the ones I had shared dreams of creating a new world with – had become yuppies. They carried mobile telephones, drove Mercedes Benz cars, and were preoccupied with making money.[50]

With *Mad Forest*, Churchill took the challenge of representing the sporadic intensity of revolution to new levels of sophistication, drew reflexive attention to the mechanisms of narrative in performance, and placed the act of spectatorship under particular pressure. The Romanian revolution may now be more than two decades away, but regime change and revolution are rarely out of the news, making *Mad Forest* an enduringly resonant and remarkable play.

Notes

1 Marcus Bauer, 'Coming to Terms with the Past: Romania', *History Today*, February 2007: 21–23.
2 M. J. Zaborowska, 'Reading the Post-Totalitarian Mind: (En)Gendering the West European Other', paper at sixth ISSEI Conference (Utrecht, 1996). As Kostova has pointed out, the end of communism has been likened to the disintegration of colonial empires: central to the perception of both is 'a crisis of self-representation involving a reshuffling and/or downright disruption of traditional dichotomies such as self/same-other, here-there, and inside-outside' (Kostova 2000: 84).
3 Pacepa (1988) has written the most famous personal account of Ceausescu's terror regime.
4 The National Council for the Study of the Securitate Files (CNSAS) was established in 1999 to shed light on the activities of high-ranking members.
5 See, for example, Ed Vulliamy, 'Notes from the Underground: Romania's Street Kids 20 Years On', *The Observer*, 9 August 2009. Some 150,000 orphans came to light after Ceausescu's fall.
6 Claire Armitstead, *Financial Times*, 27 June 1990. A legendary slogan from the time was 'Today Timisoara, tomorrow the whole country!' (Rady 1992: 101).
7 Ana Blandiana, 'A Sense of Solidarity', *Index on Censorship*, 20:1 (1991): 8. See also Anne Applebaum, *Iron Curtain: The Crushing of Eastern Europe 1944–1956* (London and New York: Allen Lane, 2012).

8 Author's public interview of Mark Wing-Davey, Dixon Theatre, University of York, 14 March 2005. See also Churchill's brief account in *Plays 3* (1998: viii).
9 Interview with Mark Wing-Davey, 14 March 2005.
10 Interview with Mark Wing-Davey, 14 March 2005.
11 Interview with Mark Wing-Davey, 14 March 2005.
12 Interview with Mark Wing-Davey, 14 March 2005.
13 Caryl Churchill interviewed by Ceridwen Thomas, 'Not Out of the Wood', *Plays and Players*, August 1990: 18–19.
14 Interview with Mark Wing-Davey, 14 March 2005.
15 Augustin Buzura, *Refuges* (Boulder, CO: Columbia University Press, 1994), p. 160.
16 Interview with Mark Wing-Davey, 14 March 2005.
17 Interview with Mark Wing-Davey, 14 March 2005.
18 Interview with Mark Wing-Davey, 14 March 2005.
19 Michael Coveney poetically referred to Act II as 'a tapestry of testimonials', *The Observer*, 8 July 1990.
20 Claire Armitstead, *Financial Times*, 27 June 1990.
21 Irving Wardle, *Independent on Sunday*, 14 October 1990.
22 Jeremy Kingston, *The Times*, 11 October 1990.
23 John Gross, *Sunday Telegraph*, 14 October 1990.
24 Interview of Mark Wing-Davey by Marc Robinson in *Village Voice*, 24 December 1991.
25 Irving Wardle, *Independent on Sunday*, 14 October 1990.
26 Kostova is referring to Tariq Ali, Howard Brenton and David Edgar. See Willcocks (2007).
27 Due to the privations of the Great Depression 'unemployed students and desperate peasants flocked to the ranks of the Iron Guard.' (Glenny 2012: 450).
28 Interview with Mark Wing-Davey, 14 March 2005.
29 Warren Leight's satirical playlet about Ceausescu's dog and its refusal to accept his master's death ends with the interrogator on all fours, a broken man, while the dog patiently waits for Ceausescu to return. 'MAN: Your master is dead!/DOG: You don't know him.' See 'The Final Interrogation of Ceausescu's Dog' in *Dark, No Sugar* (New York: Dramatists Play Service, 1992).
30 Interview with Mark Wing-Davey, 14 March 2005.
31 Interview with Mark Wing-Davey, 14 March 2005.
32 Caryl Churchill, 'To Romania with Love', *The Guardian*, 13–14 October 1990.
33 Interview with Mark Wing-Davey, 14 March 2005.
34 Interview with Mark Wing-Davey, 14 March 2005.
35 Caryl Churchill, 'To Romania with Love', *The Guardian*, 13–14 October 1990.
36 Interview with Mark Wing-Davey, 14 March 2005.

37 Caryl Churchill, 'To Romania with Love', *The Guardian*, 13–14 October 1990.
38 *Bezhti* at the Birmingham Repertory Theatre rather rocked this cosy English self-perception.
39 In fact, the broadcast went ahead.
40 Caryl Churchill, 'To Romania with Love', *The Guardian*, 13–14 October 2005.
41 Frank Rich, *New York Times*, 5 December 1991.
42 Frank Rich, *New York Times*, 5 December 1991.
43 Interview with Mark Wing-Davey, 14 March 2005.
44 Frank Rich, *New York Times*, 5 December 1991; and the same production a year later, Mel Gussow, *New York Times*, 25 January 1992.
45 Mark Wing-Davey interviewed by Marc Robinson in *Village Voice*, 24 December 1991.
46 Hong Xinyi, *The Straits Times*, 18 December 2007.
47 Peter Cochrane, *The Sydney Morning Herald*, 6 May 1993.
48 Dan Potra interviewed by Peter Cochrane, *The Sydney Morning Herald*, 6 May 1993.
49 Peter Cochrane, *The Sydney Morning Herald*, 6 May 1993.
50 Interview with Peter Cochrane, *The Sydney Morning Herald*, 6 May 1993.

7   Cross-Artform Collaborations and *Far Away*

Mad Forest marked the beginning of a decade of concentrated cross-disciplinary experiments for Churchill. She had already worked with choreographer Ian Spink on *A Mouthful of Birds* (1986) and collaborated with him again on *Lives of the Great Poisoners* (1991), *The Skriker* (1994) and *Hotel* (1997). She also developed the beginning of a productive creative partnership with composer Orlando Gough on *Great Poisoners* and *Hotel* and worked with composer Judith Weir on *The Skriker* (Aston and Diamond 2009: 71–87). The experience of *Mad Forest* appears to have intensified Churchill's disillusion with the experimental conservatism of mainstream British theatre and her frustration with the dominance of an arid realism. She turned her sights to the innovative, dynamic world of dance and physical theatre and to the extraordinary creations of international figures such as Pina Bausch at her Wuppertal dance-theatre company and Lloyd Newson, artistic director of DV8 (Climenhaga 2009; Giannachi and Luckhurst 1999).[1] Despite the fact that she had never been a conventional theatre writer, Churchill was pressed on her diversion from writing 'traditional' theatre (which to most critics seemed to mean 'realism'). She made little response to these reductive lines of enquiry, affirming her stronger interest in physical modes of expression: 'I have found the theatre a bit boring for a while, and during the time I've been tired of it, the things that have stayed with me have been from dance companies like Second Stride [Ian Spink] and DV8.'[2] In fact, Churchill, like the rising masters of physical theatre in Europe, was fascinated by learning more about physical languages of the body and by experimenting with the integration of

dialogue, sung words, music and sound scores, gesture and choreo-
graphed movement – a cross-art world that was then still more
prevalent in continental mainstream theatre than it was on British
main stages. These cross-art collaborations allowed her to work
with singers, composers, choreographers, directors and designers as
equals and her text became a single element in a medley of fused
disciplines, as opposed to the dominant organising principle (Aston
2003: 27–29). The new politics of production evidently suited her.
As she says of *Great Poisoners*:

> It's hard to visualise the show from the text alone. Long pieces
> of dance are described in a few lines of Ian's stage directions,
> and sometimes a few words are the libretto for a long passage
> of song. The whole idea of the piece and its structure were
> worked out with Ian and Orlando before I wrote any words so
> it was equally made by us all. The writer has an unfair advan-
> tage because words can easily be reproduced in a book. Ian's
> directions should be followed closely, though the detail will of
> course be different with each production. The music of *Pois-
> oners* is integral to the piece.
>
> *(Plays 3* 1998: viii)

Churchill found that these new collaborations informed her own
process in distinct ways: the need to provide fuller stage directions
to convey striking images and sequences of action gave rise to
different textual structures. Her visual imagination was permitted
freer rein because movement was accorded the same, or sometimes greater, status than the spoken word. 'Having been very
verbal for a long time', Churchill found dance stimulating to
watch, 'very moving', and 'less literal than words'.[3] It became the
director's, designer's and choreographer's joint task to flesh out
and realise interpretations of directions such as '*Pound coins come
out of her mouth*', '*The passerby never stops dancing*', '*A Sprig-
gan, grotesquely ugly and ten foot tall, having a drink*' and '*The
Kelpie and the woman who rode off on his back stroll off as
lovers*' (*The Skriker, Plays 3* 1998: 252–53, 273). Churchill was
thus liberated from having to use dialogue as her only creative
springboard and could explore wordless realms of creativity in
herself to a greater degree:

Sometimes *The Skriker* seemed like a social play with lots of characters, other times to be about just a few people. The solution I found was to have just three speaking parts, and the rest of the characters played by dancers, so that a number of stories are told but only one in words. I wrote the others as stage directions. I decided that the underworld [...] would be a more completely different world if that scene were an opera, so I wrote it as a libretto. Judith Weir then wrote the music and during rehearsal Ian Spink developed the movement from the stage directions. I'd never have written *The Skriker* that way if I hadn't already worked on other shows with dancers and singers. It brought together what had been for me two separate strands of work, plays I worked on alone and dance/music theatre pieces.

(*Plays 3* 1998: viii)

In 1997, the same year that Tony Blair and Labour finally won an election and ended 18 years of Conservative rule, Churchill enjoyed three premieres: *Hotel*, *This is a Chair* and *Blue Heart*. *Hotel* is an opera libretto, and was inspired by Churchill's image of seeing simultaneous activity in eight rooms of the same hotel. She moved comfortably between the internal and externals worlds of the figures she visualised: 'I went for few words and no sentences, just scraps of what the characters are thinking or saying' (*Plays 4* 2008: vii). She was preoccupied by questions of dialogue and audience comprehension: 'How much do we need to hear to understand what's going on?' How impatient might an audience become if denied the usual forms of verbal accessibility? (*Plays 4* 2008: vii–viii). In *This is a Chair*, directed by Stephen Daldry at the Royal Court, Churchill pushed her experiments with scene headings into a new realm by providing Brechtian frames for spectators which refused narrative relationality to the scene itself. Scene headings resonated with a suggestible media newsworthiness that acted as a distorting mirror for the dialogue that followed. How much is the spectator inferring from their own imagination? Can we ever escape the sensationalist influence of media discourse? How much is our gaze and our thinking determined by what we read and see in the news? The title is a pun on Magritte's celebrated surrealist image of a pipe bearing the words '*ceci n'est pas une pipe.*' Churchill seemed to be suggesting she may not have written a play.

> *This is a Chair* is a series of impressive subjects that a play
> might address and the scenes don't address them. […] The titles
> should probably be updated for new productions, and I'm
> happy to have suggestions run by me. Nowadays 'The War in
> Afghanistan' would probably be a title, and 'Climate Change'
> would be there. Though not, of course, written about.
>
> (*Plays 4* 2008: vii–viii)

Daldry unsettled spectators spatially by seating them on the stage to
watch actors perform on a platform above the seats of the stalls.
Scene headings were accompanied by portentous, doom-laden news
music, dubbed 'newsak' by Michael Billington, who reflected that
the piece drew attention to the disturbing dissonance between the
'cosmic issues' fired at us in the media and the banal, alarming and
increasingly surreal world that we actually inhabit.[4] Gratifyingly
for Churchill, most critics felt their flesh creep, Charles Spencer was
left chilled by 'the haunting impression of urban alienation, self-
obsession and pre-millennial tension.'[5]

Blue Heart is a pair of plays, *Heart's Desire* and *Blue Kettle*, and
was directed by Max Stafford-Clark. It opened in Bury St Edmunds
and moved to the Traverse in Edinburgh and then to the Royal Court.
Churchill acknowledged that *Hotel*, *This is a Chair* and *Blue Heart*
were written 'from a similar mindset' (*Plays 4* 2008: vii), but *Blue
Heart* took the writer's desire to deconstruct form even further: in
fact, Churchill has stated that her 'main intention' was the plays'
'destruction' (*Plays 4* 2008: viii). Originally envisioned by Stafford-
Clark 'as a satirical and epic treatment of freedom', Churchill delivered something altogether more sinister (Roberts and Stafford-Clark
2007: 175–76). Certainly, Stafford-Clark saw *Blue Heart* as an 'anti-
play' emanating from a 'distrust of and anger with theatre'.[6] Churchill
described the plays as explorations in formal self-destruct mechanisms:

> *Heart's Desire* is a play that can't happen, obsessively resetting
> itself back to the beginning every time it veers off course. *Blue
> Kettle* is a play infected with a virus.
>
> (*Plays 4* 2008: vii)

Heart's Desire is a play caught in a time loop, which repeatedly
rewinds itself to the moments just before the long-awaited arrival of

a daughter, Susy, who is returning from Australia. Her parents, Brian and Alice, her aunt Maisie, and Lewis, her brother, replay segments of dialogue and action, the actual arrival continually deferred by both realist and fantastical events: Maisie falls and injures herself, Alice reveals an affair, Alice walks out, gunmen enter and shoot them dead, a body is discovered buried in the garden, a horde of children overrun the kitchen, a ten-foot-tall bird crosses the stage, an official enters and demands their papers, a female lover of Susy's arrives. The anticipation of the arrival builds to a frenzy and the strategies to prevent it appear increasingly wayward and comic, but, at the same time, the horrific dysfunctionality of the family becomes ever more manifest. In *Blue Kettle*, Derek deceives elderly women into believing that he was the son they gave up for adoption 40 years earlier but, as the women become more emotionally distraught, the language of Churchill's play breaks down and the words 'kettle' and 'blue' start to infect the dialogue with increasing frequency, gradually collapsing into a dénouement infested with syllables and letters. Stafford-Clark's producer felt the plays were 'all about a writer's journey', Stafford-Clark himself that they behaved like a recalcitrant horse with a mind of its own (Roberts 2008: 142). Critics thought it a work of technical genius and were intrigued:

> *Heart's Desire* is like rifling through off-cuts in the writer's wastepaper basket and seeing what happened when the characters were let loose.[7]

'Nightmarishly difficult' for the actors to remember and enact, Bernard Gallagher recalled his work on the premiere as 'the most challenging job I'd ever had' (Roberts 2008: 253). Stafford-Clark had to work out a rehearsal method for it and how to overcome the technical problems he felt the play quite deliberately posed (Roberts 2008: 252). *Heart's Desire* also baffled interpreters.[8] Among other things, it has been accused of being an experiment in 'form for form's sake', described as a meditation on the fear of death, and a purely technical exercise in laying bare the multifarious routes an author might take in developing a narrative.[9] It may be all of these. In fact, the internal combustion of the structure matches the family's repetition compulsion and suggests the daughter's return cannot be faced because of a pre-existing trauma. Why are family members in a state of arrested hysteria over Susy's return? The body in the garden stands for the skeleton in the family cupboard. The father seems especially implicated: he originally initiates the cyclical structures and he is most anxious about her arrival and why she might be delayed. The parents are bound up in a primal conflict over their daughter's affections and Lewis, the brother, desperately wants to name the trauma but is repeatedly banished by his parents and anaesthetises himself with alcohol: 'It's time we had it out. It's time we spoke the truth. [...] I want my life to begin' (*Plays 4* 2008: 83). The father has always favoured his daughter, in ways that have aroused the intense suspicion of the other family members; 'Dad knows where she is, don't you dad? Daddy always knows where Susy is' (*Plays 4* 2008: 71).

Freud's repetition compulsion posits that an individual may unconsciously be in such unbearable pain that they repeat a fixed pattern of destructive behaviour in order to re-find the repressed material and experience it in the present. The drive to repeat stems from a need to achieve mastery over a traumatic situation from the past, to transform an event that was endured into one that is over-come, but the problem is that repetition compulsion is doomed to a cycle of continued failures (Freud 1955).[10] Many psychoanalytic theorists recognise that repetition and re-enactment are common occurrences in the lives of individuals who experienced sexual abuse as children (Russell 2006; Bowins 2010: 289). The compulsion is reproduced not as a memory but as an action, and the individual repeats it without knowing it. As Russell has argued, repetition compulsion is a form of death drive:

> The repetition compulsion murders time; the repetition com-pulsion is suicidal. To the extent that we experience the present in terms only of the past, to the degree that we murder present time and opportunity by persistently, malignantly demonstrat-ing that there is no possible difference between the past and the present, to that degree we cease to live. [...] every repetition contains a nucleus of hate.
>
> (Russell 2006: 611)

Churchill borrows a psychoanalytic idea and deploys it as both form and content. But what is the family trauma? The choice of repetition compulsion in itself implies childhood sexual abuse and the fact that when Susy arrives, in two separate sequences at the end, the father blurts out: 'You are my heart's desire' and 'You are my heart's–' strongly suggests the family's terrible secret (*Plays 4* 2008: 92, 95). Russell describes repetition compulsion as:

> malignantly uneducatable [...]. It is as if there is some systematic internal bug, some glitch that results in the individual being helpless against his or her repetitions. It is as if the person, despite what they might avow, goes out in search of, arranges, in a profoundly uncanny way, a repeat of something very painful
> (Russell 2006: 606)

The whole family is trapped in a continued enactment of a repressed trauma. The father's confession of the desire to self-cannibalise mirrors the play's own autophagic form (*Plays 4* 2008: 81): the plot and structure swallow themselves up repeatedly. In his thesis *Difference and Repetition*, Gilles Deleuze asserts that repetition disguises itself in constituting itself: the repeated cannot be represented, but can only be signified, masked by what signifies it, and itself masking what it signifies (Deleuze 1994). Williams, an interpreter of Deleuze's theory, claims that:

> A theatre of repetition is opposed to the theatre of representation, just as movement is opposed to the concept and to representation which refers it back to the concept. In the theatre of repetition we experience pure forces, dynamic lines in space which act without intermediary on the spirit, and link it directly with nature and history, with a language which speaks before word, with gestures which develop before organised bodies, with masks before faces, with spectres and phantoms before characters – the whole apparatus of repetition as a 'terrible power.'
> (Williams 2003: 10)

Churchill's self-consuming play with its appalling incestuous secrets is a brilliant example of her quest for a model that is in itself the thing it demonstrates – a complex complementarity of form and content, its engine ceaselessly turning itself over and threatening to burn itself out.

Hauntology and the visceral

Frameworks for effectively interrogating Churchill's fusion of disciplines, notion of perceptual simultaneity and interest in creating moments of sensory overload for the spectator, are only slowly emerging. One vocabulary currently underexplored in relation to Churchill's plays of the 1990s is spectrality (Del Pilar Blanco and Peeren 2013): ghosts, the living dead, reanimations of fictional figures and versions of the undead abound throughout her plays and act as a contrapuntal narrative of the uncanny in dialogue with the material, embodied world.[11] Churchill's use of dance and gestural theatre, music and song all relate to her preoccupation with the absent presence of the Other – whether suggestive of the oppressed and rightless, or of the traumatic present finding echoes in forgotten and invisible histories. *The Skriker*, which Churchill frequently referred to as her 'fairy play' (Roberts 2008: 247), relies more than any other of her plays on evocations of the supernatural and the continual interplay of the everyday with an extra-sensory world visible to the spectator but not necessarily to the human characters on stage.

In *The Skriker* Churchill consciously extends her investigation of permissible visibility. The spectre, as Derrida has made clear in his theory of hauntology, symbolises the politically marginal and is a disruptive force: it signifies 'the visibility of the invisible' and a thing 'beyond the phenomenon'; it is 'what one imagines, what one thinks one sees and which one projects' (Derrida 2006: 124). The relation to the historical disempowerment and silencing of women and Churchill's many ghostly female figures are clear. The magical appearances and disappearances of the Skriker, her shape-shifting and spell-casting, and her jumbled, visceral poetics of speech indicate a primordial energy and earth force – as Churchill describes it in her stage directions she is a 'death portent, ancient and damaged' (*Plays 3* 1998: 243). At the same time, the Skriker's need to feed off young female humans and possess their new-borns encodes a post-Freudian symbolic of danger and destructiveness that is externalised by her vulnerable victims, teenagers Josie and Lily who are social and economic outcasts – and the hapless, alienated ghosts of late twentieth-century Western democracy. In *Heart's Desire* Susy is the revenant locked in a projected limbo always in the act of returning but who never finally arrives, the signifier of an abuse and incest narrative, whose return is a Derridean perpetual 'conjuring away' by family and society (Derrida 2006: 120). In *Blue Kettle* the spectres are both the elderly ghost-mothers whom Derek seeks to deceive into believing that they gave him up for adoption as a baby so that he might rook them financially, and his actual mother who is represented in one short scene and confined to a geriatric ward. Derek blithely confesses his ruthless con-tricks to his real mother in the knowledge that her Alzheimer's disease or dementia has rendered her a cognitive cripple. Unable to negotiate the present, Derek's mother is caught somewhere between memory and fantasy, a species of the living dead who has already passed some unseen threshold. In light of this scene Derek's compulsion to search out surrogate mothers also appears to be driven by an unconscious belief that he might find a connection to his absent, emotionally unavailable mother. But in another sense, Derek seems to be the revenant, both haunted and self-haunting and paradoxically the most vivid characters are Derek's fake mothers. In *Hotel*, Churchill's Ghost of scene 12 is without memory and does not know why he or she haunts (the gender is not specified and gender may too be something forgotten); the trauma is the perpetual longing to be seen, the entrapment of place, and the state of invisibility – any former life has evaporated into a memoryless, eternal present, a representation that explodes Derrida's 'phantomatic mode of production' because the haunted do not appear to apprehend the revenant's presence and without apprehension the revenant has no identity (Derrida 2006: 120). However, the spectator inhabits a territory of double alienation since he or she apprehends the seen and unseen, becoming, in effect, a seer: if, as Derrida argues 'politicians are seers or visionaries' who 'desire and fear an apparition which they know will not present anyone in person but will strike a series of blows to be delivered' then the spectator becomes the political viewer and the actors the visitants. In a sense, given the rituals of theatre, both actor and spectator also become revenants.

Derrida's hauntology maps the suppression of a Marxist politics in the democratic West and suggests other spectral landscapes that signify the voiceless and disempowered. 'Ghosts hover where secrets are held in time: the secrets of what has been unspoken, unacknowledged', states Alice Rayner (2006: x). Ghosts on stage are also a self-referential metaphor for the act of viewing and constitute the theatrical paradox of absent presence (Luckhurst and Morin 2014). Derrida's theory of spectrality inherently requires the existence of matter and theatre contains the same paradox of the material formation of the immaterial, and the actor's plastic construction of 'character' and 'narrative' from the body in space.

Hauntology and theories of embodiment suggest a useful terrain for future explorations of Churchill's cross-art productions. In *(Syn) aesthetics: Redefining Visceral Theatre*, Machon (2009) has begun to try and describe the visceral exploration at the heart of Churchill's (among others) more recent theatre works. Machon defines (syn)aesthetics as 'performance work which constantly resists and explodes established forms and concepts', as 'always open to developments in contemporary practice and analysis [...] it shifts between performance disciplines, just as it shifts between the sensual and the intellectual, the somatic (affecting the body or absorbed through the body) and the semantic (the mental reading of signs)' (Machon 2009: 4). (Syn)aesthetics has a shapeshift morphology, 'its only constant being the fused somatic/semantic manner of its performative style and subsequent audience response' (Machon 2009: 4). Machon also defines the dominance of 'the body as text in performance and an unusual rendering of verbal speech to establish a visceral-verbal *play*text' (Machon 2009: 4). While Machon makes some interesting points, her work is unfortunately underpinned by the same mind-body dualism that plagues much theorisation of embodiment: the verbal, for example, is constructed as separate from the somatic despite the fact that words are unavoidably produced by the physical body (unless generated wholly by technology). Linda Bassett, a well-known Churchill actress, describes the effect of sensory overload on an audience:

> I often find with Caryl's plays that when people try to follow them with their head – they get stuck [...] If you sit there and let her work on you, you get the experience. But people who fight it and try and make sense of it get stuck and then say this doesn't make sense.
>
> (Machon 2009: 144)

Following the vocal narrative alone, argues Bassett, will not render the piece accessible in the way we are accustomed to with certain forms of conventional stage play. Instead, Churchill is searching for a viscerally immediate theatre that does not proceed from realist logic. This is as true of the overlapping dialogue in the first act of *Top Girls*, as it is of the dance and movement sequences in *Lives of the Great Poisoners*, *The Skriker*, *Hotel* and the fractured repetitions of *Blue Heart*. Similarly, Churchill's, at times, dense poetic wordplay and increasing penchant for which the elliptical do not conform to codified forms of dramatic logic but find their meaning in the feelings aroused in the spectator by the carefully composed, often surprising juxtapositions of body, sound and image. In the languages of movement and the body, of the supernatural and magical, Churchill moves even further away from stage naturalism and defamiliarises audiences with what they think they know about theatre and stage representation, finding alternative modes of exploring the appearance and making of political theatre. The exploration of Churchill's cross-artforms through hauntology and embodiment offers a way of excavating her specific worlds of the uncanny, and in Alice Rayner's words allows 'a sensation of seeing for the first time what one has seen many times before' (Rayner 2006: xix).

Terror and catastrophe: *Far Away*

Far Away is Churchill's most chilling play and, tellingly, was premiered in the year of the new millennium. For Churchill it marked the end of a phase of experimenting with self-implosive form; as she has said, '*Far Away* feels to me quite different as the play isn't being undermined' (*Plays 4* 2008: viii) – but it is, nonetheless, an experiment in finding a dystopian form for a dystopian content. It contains three stylistically distinct acts and moves from a domestic interior in Act I, to a totalitarian setting in Act II, and a world of apocalyptic conflict in Act III, in which humans, animals, matter and energy forces are all locked in the war to end all wars, and planet Earth is in self-destructive freefall. In the words of John Peter: '*Far Away* is a terrible play, in the Yeatsian sense of a terrible beauty – you emerge shaken. There's nothing else like this play.'[12]

The usual critical frame for *Far Away* categorises it within Churchill's longstanding interest in ecology and the growing evidence that we are destroying our natural habitat (Rabillard 1998:

88–104). Aston argues that it is 'a cautionary tale, not least for feminism' and depicts the inculcation of catastrophic violence within a system of ideologies which all lead to meaningless chaos (Aston 2003: 36). For Elin Diamond, *Far Away*'s most shocking feature is its representation of an environment where a humane moral sensibility has been completely annihilated; in its place stands a 'grotesque topography – a war of all against all with no sign of resistance or memory of an ethical alternative' (Aston and Diamond 2009: 139). Rabillard also finds that, at its heart, *Far Away* is an interrogation of ethics, examining the common rehearsals of utilitarian and aesthetic cases for genocide or war put forward by politicians or war-leaders to justify acts of aggression (Rabillard 1998: 101). The recent origins of dramatic examinations of 'nihilism's ethical possibilities,' argues Ken Urban, can be traced back to the work in 'in-yer-face' dramatists such as Sarah Kane in the 1990s (Urban 2004: 355).

More recently, *Far Away* has been theorised within a body of contemporary plays that confront both the rhetoric and political strategy of 'terror' and address the failure of Western democracy in theory and practice (Brady 2012). It is now accepted that climate change and terror go hand in hand, since, in parts of the world where health and well-being are most affected by climate change, the likelihood of conflict increases exponentially (Richardson et al 2011:123). President George Bush coined the term 'War on Terror' in the wake of the terrorist attacks on New York in 2001; it refers to an international campaign, led by the United States, to eliminate militant Islamists and jihadists. Acts of terror such as the attacks on the World Trade Center have come to be perceived as acts that typify twenty-first-century global warfare in the West and have changed the terms of military engagement. Jenny Hughes has written persuasively about both Churchill's and Mark Ravenhill's dramatic experiments 'with the excremental powers of the voice [...] to materialise and critique the exceptional realities of war' (Hughes 2011: 120). According to Hughes, the syntactical and linguistic distortions in Act III of *Far Away* signify:

> The failure of the democratic voice to expel and excise the violence and atrocity of war. [...] such distortions of speech and confusing modalities of being enact an ethical imperative to

pay attention to the violence obscured by rational voices in the public sphere.

(Hughes 2011: 121)

For Hughes, Churchill's use of the linguistically and visually surreal becomes a means of highlighting the 'political fictions of democracy' and 'in this doubling of fictions, a fictional order's doubling and deadly effects are revealed' (Hughes 2011: 121). It is also productive to read *Far Away* against Naomi Klein's controversial book *The Shock Doctrine: The Rise of Disaster Capitalism* (Klein 2007), once described as 'the master narrative of our time'.[13] According to Klein, global corporations have forced Milton Friedman's free market policies onto vulnerable countries recovering from disasters or upheavals in order to secure economic and ideological domination. The occupation of Iraq, Klein asserts, is the most comprehensive implementation of the shock doctrine ever attempted. In *Far Away* the actual instigators of the atrocity remain off-stage throughout, but their power in Acts I and II is pervasive, and in Act III the result is Total War.

London and New York premieres: the Bosnian War and 9/11

Tantalised by reports of horror, audiences flocked to see Stephen Daldry's interpretation of *Far Away* at the Royal Court in 2000. Indeed, the ghoulish demand was so great that there were two showings a night (made possible by the running time of under an hour). Daldry also directed the New York premiere (2002). For the Royal Court, he cast Linda Bassett as Harper, Annabelle Seymour-Julen as young Joan, Katherine Tozer as older Joan, and Kevin McKidd as Todd; for the New York Theater Workshop production, he cast celebrated actress, Frances McDormand as Harper, Alexa Eisenstein as young Joan, Marin Ireland as older Joan, and Chris Messina as Todd.

For European audiences in 2000 the backdrop to *Far Away* was the Bosnian War. The clandestine, violent internment of individuals and their transportation at night had strong resonances of both the genocides of the Holocaust and the ethnic cleansing of Bosnian Muslims in Bosnia-Herzegovina during the 1990s (Glenny 2012: 634–62). The Bosnian War was the most deadly conflict in

Europe since World War II: more than 2,100,000 were displaced by Serb and Croat forces in a bid to create ethnically homogenous territories, and more than 100,000 were killed. The inactivity of United Nations' peace-keeping officials, notoriously reduced to standing by as 8,000 Bosnians were murdered at Srebrenica, an internationally agreed 'safe area,' generated a lasting crisis about humanitarian aid and negotiation (Vulliamy 1994). News of torture, mass killing, the systematic rape of women and the discovery of concentration camps only 50 years after Europeans thought they would never see such atrocity on their soil again, was as shocking as the paralysis of Western powers in confronting the scale of the problem (Vulliamy 1999). Western governments' refusal to intervene has been the subject of intense scrutiny and peace study scholars subsequently developed new theories on complicity and the typologies and responsibilities of 'bystanders to genocide' (Vetlesen 2000; Subotic 2011). Obliquely, *Far Away* drew on a ghastliness that was close to home. As Max Stafford-Clark saw it, Churchill had 'developed her own response to a political agenda which she has discovered she cannot effectively address directly any more. The play is compressed and surreal but epic' (Roberts 2008: 146).

The three acts of *Far Away* are linked by the figure of Joan, a girl of unspecified age in Act I; probably a late teenager and portrayed in a working environment in Act II; and a young woman, hardened to the rigours of slaughtering anything and anyone who threatens her survival in Act III. Act I plays brilliantly off its fairy-tale trope: a new arrival at her aunt and uncle's house, Joan cannot sleep and comes down to the kitchen at dead of night to seek solace from her aunt, Harper. The child is evidently anxious, and under cunning interrogation from Harper ingenuously reveals that she climbed down the tree outside her window, discovered a lorry and watched her uncle beating 'people' with a stick and bundling them into a shed. Joan asks her aunt why some people, including children, had blood on their faces and why there was 'so much blood' (*Plays 4* 2008: 138). Harper expertly persuades Joan that her uncle was only striking 'traitors' and that he is secretly a hero, enabling endangered victims to escape (*Plays 4* 2008: 141). The spine-chilling quality of the scene deepens as the child is snared ever more in Harper's net of lies, painfully unaware of any danger to herself. Churchill's pacing of the information flow offers a master-class in plotting and the art of suspense, and playwright David Edgar has described Act I as 'one of the most stunningly crafted dramatic scenes ever written'.[14] By the end of the act, Joan has become an unwitting recruit to the barbarism, agreeing to help Harper 'clean up in the morning' (*Plays 4* 2008: 142), corrupted by the rhetoric of doing her patriotic duty for a moral cause.

HARPER: You're part of a big movement now to make things better. You can be proud of that. You can look at the stars and think here we are in our little bit of space, and I'm on the side of the people who are putting things right, and your soul will expand right into the sky.

(*Plays 4* 2008: 142)

Stephen Daldry made his name with his expressionist West End hit of Priestley's morality play *An Inspector Calls*, and his film of the working-class boy turned classical ballet dancer *Billy Elliot*. Visually daring and politically driven, Daldry's agenda was in sympathy with Churchill's and his direction of *This is a Chair* had cemented a mutual interest in exploring poetic stage images. His directing instincts 'encourage performers to find physical ways to unlock the emotion of a scene,' and matched Churchill's increasing focus on the body (Aston and Diamond 2009: 158). Wendy Lesser has described his technique as:

physical-actioning: rather than work on lines in terms of 'actioned moments', he encourages actors to explore gestures and movement to highlight or counterpoint dialogue so that a line, a moment or a scene embody meaning. This process is a route to the visual and the experiential qualities that characterise his style of production.

(Lesser 1997: 146)

Lesser's focus on counterpoint is especially interesting in relation to *Far Away*, since Churchill's use of irony is so particular: by the end the characters have been conditioned to behave as killing machines and their moral universe is one of normalised massacre. It is the gap between the characters' perception of their world and the spectator's horror at what they have become that Daldry exploited with such creative ingenuity. Daldry's choice to cast two actors to play Joan, a child and an adult woman, was a means of emphasising both Joan's innocent vulnerability and the fact that her recruitment as an accomplice to atrocity is initiated by an adult caregiver: the two bodies demonstrated the transformation from girlish puppy-fat to the rigid, flexed muscles of a warrior.

Designer Ian MacNeil's painted frontcloth, which greeted spectators in London and New York, depicted a delusory idyll of a chocolate-box cottage nestled among wooded hills. This was raised to reveal a stark interior of a rocking chair and a kitchen table, as Harper sewed in the lamplight, singing to herself in a costume reminiscent of the 1930s and the ascent of Hitler. Joan entered in a costume from a child's storybook, wearing a white nightdress and carrying a shabby teddy bear, a picture of innocence – although not for long. When MacNeil's frontcloth was lowered at the end its phoney image was a travesty of what had, in fact, been seen.[15]

The shattered ideal had particular meaning for audiences at the New York Theater Workshop only a year after 9/11 and the devastating terrorist attack on the World Trade Center in which nearly 3,000 were killed and more than 6,000 injured. Ben Brantley noted that Paul Arditti's sound design lulled spectators into a false sense of security with a 'drowsy humming' and 'murmur of flowing water' as the frontcloth rose.[16]

> For New Yorkers living in the elongated shadow of September 11th, the waking dreamscape of *Far Away*, where the promise of violence broods even in the cosiest corners, is bound to feel familiar. Ms Churchill envisions a world in which nothing, but nothing, is to be trusted.[17]

For Brantley, Frances McDormand's 'brilliant, fractionally precise timing', which involved holding a suspect, 'careful pause' before each of her replies to Joan's litany of questions, 'turned the everyday into a brush with the apocalypse'.[18] In many ways, 9/11 had already given Americans a sense of what the end of a world might feel like and Churchill's 'dramaturgy of terror', as Diamond has observed, was all too real (Aston and Diamond 2009: 125–43).

The artist as collaborator

In Act II Joan has just qualified as a professional milliner, and creates a prize-winning hat in her first week. In six short scenes she and fellow-worker, Todd, who has made nearly 300 hats, fall in love, share as many intimacies as they dare, and discuss their artistic persuasions. But their exchanges are uneasy, the hats utterly absurd and impractical, and they appear to be under constant surveillance and terrified of being overheard.

Paul Arditti's sound-scape amplified and distorted the noises of scissors cutting and fabric being torn, creating a gruesomely

Figure 7.1 Fiona Cooper in *Far Away*, York Theatre Royal © Mary Luckhurst

suggestive backdrop of terror. Todd and Joan, it emerges, are part
of a workforce employed to design and make hats for prisoners who
are forced to parade in them on their way to execution. Far from
expressing any concern about the mass killings, both are consumed
by their poor pay and conditions, Joan ignores the show trials on
television, and finds it regrettable that the hats are destroyed:

JOAN: Its seems so sad to burn them with the bodies.
TODD: No I think that's the joy of it. The hats are ephemeral. It's
        like a metaphor for something or other.
JOAN: Well, life.

(*Plays 4* 2008: 150)

This blackly ironic exchange reveals that their artistic output exists
only to humiliate and depersonalise those on a march to their
extermination. Joan and Todd are desensitised and lack all empathy, providing the accessories to the carnival death costume; artistic
'meaning' is found in a sick joke celebrating the massacre of the
unwanted. Art is yoked to the service of a killing machine, a narrative familiar from artists such as Leni Riefenstahl who enjoyed
the patronage of Hitler (Bach 2008). In this perverse world, the
greater art is the killing itself, and the artist's 'self-expression' is
controlled and deployed to serve the project of 'cleansing' a nation,
although the artists themselves have no insight into their complicity.
Daldry's direction in these scenes emphasised the murderousness of
creation as the actors stuck pins, stretched material, and stabbed
and ripped fabric with scissors. Bearing out Hannah Arendt's and
Daniel Goldhagen's theories of National Socialists' obsession with
obedience, the actors performed Todd and Joan as classic examples
of the banality of evil: as two workers just doing their jobs – which
happen to involve the annihilation of other human beings (Arendt
1998; Goldhagen 1997).

The prisoners appear once in the most significant scene of the
play, and are described in just three sentences. Churchill advises
using as many bodies as possible, preferably 100 (*Plays 4* 2008: 132).

Act II.5
*Next day. A procession of ragged, beaten, chained prisoners,
each wearing a hat, on their way to execution. The finished*

hats are even more enormous and preposterous than in the previous scene.

(*Plays 4* 2008: 149)

The only change in Daldry's technical team for the New York show was the costume designer. In London Iona Kendrick's hats suggested the indulgence and wealth of the leisured classes; in New York Catherine Zuber effected an 'astonishing coup de théâtre' by pushing aesthetic boundaries far more towards the outlandish grand statement.[19] Zuber's creations created a giddy conflict in the spectator between the desire to allow the art to amaze and the inclination to suppress one's horror; Kendrick's hats emphasised the division of material power between victim and perpetrator. Daldry cast about 30 performers, ranging from children to the physically frail and elderly. They dragged themselves into view, chained together, their broken bodies a stark contrast with their extravagantly beautiful and surreal headgear. For Irving Wardle the play suddenly exploded into 'a mass spectacle with line after line of manacled

Figure 7.2 The Parade Scene, *Far Away*, York Theatre Royal © Mary Luckhurst

prisoners shuffling towards execution, clad in hats beyond the craziest fantasies of Ascot'.[20] Arditti's sound-score reverberated with abusive, baying crowds to complete an image of stark denigration and hopelessness. 'This is a shocking moment,' wrote Charles Spencer, 'recalling the horrors of the Nazi camps.'[21] But *Far Away* was not that far away: only a year earlier a journalist, Ed Vulliamy, had reported on a concentration camp in Omarska, Bosnia:

> Nothing could have prepared us for what we saw as we entered. [...] A column of men were drilled across the yard by uniformed guards. They were horribly thin – the bones of their pencil-thin elbows and wrists protruded like pieces of jagged stone through parchment skin. [...] Prisoners, who survived by drinking their own and each other's urine, were forever being called out of their cramped quarters by name. Some would return caked in blood, bruised and wounded by knives; others would never be seen alive again. Squads of inmates were ordered to load corpses onto trucks. [...] The day after we 'discovered' Omarska, it was quickly closed and the prisoners transferred so that prying international eyes would not uncover these secrets.
>
> (Vulliamy 1999: 608)

For the New York theatre community, a large constituency of which is Jewish, the reminders of the Holocaust were mixed with the fear of terrorism. London audiences were more susceptible to questions of individual and collective responsibility because of the failure of liberal interventionism in Bosnia: 'Daldry spares us no atrocity and none of the blame,' wrote Sam Marlowe.[22] But, understandably, post-9/11 New Yorkers identified with Joan's loss of innocence and immersion in carnage.

In Act III Joan returns to Harper's house to see Todd, who is now her husband. Joan describes a journey through a shattered ecosystem that has unleashed war on itself. Everything has been recruited and identifies itself with a different faction: ants, Latvian dentists, the Chileans, the weather, rivers, mountains, silence, light, cats, dogs, butterflies, children under five, musicians. The list proliferates endlessly. Churchill's language conveys a surreal, prosaic acceptance of extreme horror, an environmental apocalypse, and a landscape overrun with death and destruction. Killing is an every-day and meaningless act and can be effected by human, animal, plant, matter or energy force. Life has been reduced to obliterating anything and anyone. Churchill ends the play with a terrifying and eloquent monologue by Joan, now an unthinking and practised murderer:

> Of course birds saw me, everyone saw me walking along but nobody knew why, I could have been on a mission, everyone's moving about and no one knows why, and in fact I killed two cats and a child under five so it wasn't that different from a mission [...] I'll go on to the end after this. It wasn't so much the birds I was frightened of, it was the weather, the weather here's on the side of the Japanese.
>
> (*Plays 4* 2008: 158)

Thus Churchill has mapped Joan's journey from child's innocence to state-sponsored killer for a cause she never understood and which is now lost in all-out carnage – a sombre dramatic arc for the new millennium.

Notes

1 Churchill was also influenced by the English National Opera's experimental production of *The Seven Deadly Sins* in 1979; see Claire Armitstead, *The Guardian*, 12 January 1994.
2 Claire Armitstead, *The Guardian*, 12 January 1994.
3 Caryl Churchill interviewed by Judith Mackrell, *The Guardian*, 20 January 1994.
4 Michael Billington, *The Guardian*, 26 June 1997.
5 Charles Spencer, *Daily Telegraph*, 27 June 1997.
6 Max Stafford-Clark interviewed by Matt Wolf, *New York Times*, 31 January 1999.
7 Georgina Brown, *Mail on Sunday*, 5 October 1997.
8 Author's interview with Max Stafford-Clark, Dixon Theatre, University of York, 8 December 2004.
9 Neil Cooper, *The Times*, 25 August 1997; Paul Taylor, *The Independent*, 25 September 1997; Nick Curtis, *Evening Standard*, 22 August 1997.
10 Repetitive maladaptive behaviour is currently the main reason people seek psychotherapy. Brad Bowins, 'Repetitive Maladaptive Behaviour:

Beyond Repetition Compulsion', *The American Journal of Psychoanalysis*, vol. 70 (2010): 282.

11 Freud's definition of the uncanny incorporates 'that class of the frightening which leads back to what is known of old and long familiar', 'the idea of being robbed of one's eyes' and 'uncertainty whether an object is living or inanimate'. See Freud (1955: vol. 17, 220, 230).

12 John Peter, *Sunday Times*, 3 December 2000.

13 John Gray, 'The End of the World as We Know It', *Guardian*, 19 September 2007.

14 David Edgar, in conversation, 'Theatre and Ghosts' conference, University of York, 1 July 2011.

15 Author's notes from seeing production.

16 Ben Brantley, *New York Times*, 12 November 2002.

17 Ben Brantley, *New York Times*, 12 November 2002.

18 Ben Brantley, *New York Times*, 12 November 2002.

19 Ben Brantley, *New York Times*, 12 November 2002.

20 Irving Wardle, *Sunday Telegraph*, 3 December 2000.

21 Charles Spencer, *Daily Telegraph*, 5 December 2000.

22 Sam Marlowe, *What's On*, 6 December 2000.

Part V

Churchill in the Twenty-First Century

8 Key Production: *A Number*

The hinterland to Churchill's futuristic experiment, *A Number* (2002), was mapped by the intense, often explosive debates about human cloning that broke onto the international stage of genetic science in the late 1990s.

In 1997 Ian Wilmut and Keith Campbell at the Roslin Institute in Scotland announced that they had cloned the first sheep, Dolly, from an enucleated adult donor cell. Dolly's existence was a biological breakthrough. In rapid pursuit, scientists from around the world announced the successful cloning of mice, pigs, Elsie the cow, Ralph the rat, and CC the cat.[1] Dolly became an overnight media sensation, fuelling worldwide concerns about the potential abuses of human cloning and sparking a storm of political, legal, ethical and religious debates that continue until this day.[2] President Clinton took immediate steps to ban federal funding for research into human cloning and asked the National Bioethics Advisory Commission to make policy recommendations. All scientifically advanced countries have since introduced laws regulating cloning and the discipline of 'new genetics' (which includes the now even more controversial territory of stem cell research),[3] and the European Union and United Nations have implemented international agreements (Brannigan 2001; Macintosh 2013). Dolly, meanwhile, has won extraordinary celebrity status and 'Dollymania' shows little sign of abating for, as Sarah Franklin attests in her witty book, *Dolly Mixtures*, 'few animals have so succinctly embodied the complexity of human purposes and directions' (Franklin 2007: 13). Wilmut and Campbell have argued that Dolly ushered in 'the second creation', a new 'age of biological control' (Wilmut et al

2000), and Franklin has asserted that Dolly's importance as a cultural signifier of new forms of scientific intervention and experiment cannot be overestimated:

> as the founder animal not only of a new form of reproduction (transgenesis) but for a novel realignment of the biological, cultural, political, and economic relations that connect humans, animals, technologies, markets and knowledges [...], Dolly's existence can be seen to redefine the limits of the biological, with implications for both how sex and reproduction are understood and practised.
>
> (Franklin 2007: 2–3, 5)

It is not hard to see why Churchill, with her long-held interest in the politics of sexuality and reproduction, and her fascination with identity, family and social environment, found the subject of biological engineering so creatively provocative; nor to see why Churchill might enjoy the role-play challenges she could set actors through the subject of cloning.

Lee Silver traces the modern usage of 'clone' back to 1903, when it was invented to refer to a colony or organisms created asexually from a single ancestor, and establishes that, as originally defined, it referred to a large number of organisms.[4] In the past hundred years, science fiction novelists, graphic artists and Hollywood producers have successfully exploited widespread cultural anxiety about human cloning, as well as bolstered its attendant popular myths, many of which are aired in Churchill's play. The films *The Boys from Brazil* (1978), which treats the cloning of Adolf Hitler; *Star Wars II: Attack of the Clones* (2002) and various episodes from the television series *Star Trek* and *X-Files* all famously deal with the imagined horrors of cloning, and there are numerous other examples (see Macintosh 2013: 79).[5] Cloning remains a hot topic. In December 2002 the Raelians, a sect who believe that the human race was begotten by aliens 25,000 years ago, announced the birth of the first human clone but no evidence was produced to support their claim and it was dismissed as a publicity stunt. In Britain, the creation of cloned babies is forbidden (as it is in most European countries) under the Human Fertilisation and Embryology Act (1990), although, controversially, the creation of human embryos up to the age of 14 days is permitted for research and therapeutic development. Objections to cloning are predominantly ethical and religious, and for some human cloning is akin to taboos such as incest (Brannigan 2001: 203). Much contemporary science has a metaphysical background with radical utilitarian connotations: it is founded on the belief that utility should constitute the main criterion according to which we should guide the evolution and progress of our scientific endeavours, but for many cloning is a highly emotive subject.

The imposter fallacy

The metaphysical, legal and ethical debates surrounding human cloning are complex and much public opinion has been influenced by uninformed media scaremongering. Kerry Lynn Macintosh posits four prevalent fallacies, which provide a useful contextual backdrop to *A Number*. The 'identity fallacy' asserts that a clone is an exact copy of his or her genetic predecessor (Macintosh 2013: 69–101). In fact, a clone, is only genetically identical to the donor, and the scientific consensus is that genetic material determines only a portion of the total amount of the properties that an organism possesses. Scientists have proved that genes alone do not predetermine an individual's looks, forecast their health problems or condition what they will think or how they will live. After birth, genetics and environmental factors inextricably inform each other, and an individual's interaction with environment is, by definition, unique. Despite the scientific evidence that animal clones do not exactly resemble their donor or each other, the popular fear is that human clones would suffer what Macintosh calls 'diminished individuality' (Macintosh 2013: 86), based on the misconception that clones' looks, cognitive function and personality would match their genetic donor's. Like B2 in *A Number*, it is assumed that the clone would manifest identity dysphoria and suffer trauma. As the title of Churchill's play suggests, identity fallacy tends to be accompanied by the fear of innumerability and eugenic cloning, an assumption that human clones would be produced in large numbers, giving rise to clone armies and loss of human diversity (Macintosh 2013: 86–90). The 'artefact fallacy' asserts the objectification of human clones as 'unnatural', designer-made products manufactured in artificial wombs: this is a favourite narrative thread for much science fiction (Macintosh 2013: 103–23). In the opening dialogue of *A Number*, Salter, the donor father, is corrected by one of his sons, B2, for referring to his cloned siblings as 'things' (*Plays 4* 2008: 165). But B2 rapidly reveals his psychic implosion at the news:

SALTER: sorry I said things, I didn't mean anything by that, it just
B2:   no forget it, it's nothing, it's
SALTER: because of course for me you're the
B2:   yes I know what you meant, I just, because of course I
           want them to be things, I do think they're things, I don't
           think they're, of course I *do* think they're them just as
           much as I'm me but I. I don't know what I think, I feel
           terrible.

                                                    (*Plays 4* 2008: 167)

The very existence of his cloned siblings unstitches B2's sense of selfhood. Macintosh's 'imposter fallacy' is also implicit in Churchill's opening. The imposter fallacy posits the idea of a sinister 'impersonator who is visually indistinguishable from the DNA donor', who exploits his or her likeness to others through assuming a false identity and stealing assets, jobs and loved ones (Macintosh 2013: 131). B2 is already in doubt about his uniqueness and authenticity, although ironically will later discover he is himself a clone and potentially an 'imposter':

B2:   what if someone else is the one, the first one, the real one
           and I'm [...]
SALTER: So you didn't suddenly see
B2:   what suddenly see myself coming round the corner

        [...]

B2:   don't they say you die if you meet yourself?
SALTER: walk round the corner and see yourself you could get a
           heart attack. Because if that's me over there who am I?
B2:   Yes but it's not me over there

                                              (*Plays 4* 2008: 166, 170)

Macintosh's 'resurrection fallacy' holds that 'a person can be cloned to extend or resume the life of a deceased genetic predecessor [...] as a means of achieving immortality and raising the dead' (Macintosh 2013: 147). This might have positive or negative ramifications. Might a parent choose to try and resurrect a dead child and then be disappointed or treat the child as a commodity? Would cloned children result in family dysfunctionality? Suppose a particular community sought to make multiple clones of a charismatic leader or a dictator? What would a clone feel about his or her resurrection and the negation of the self, or a self that is presumed to be inherently 'other'? In these scenarios the clone is understood to claim the lost life and sometimes even to possess the same memory bank. Salter, it is later revealed, was trying to replace his once 'perfect' young son, B1, who, in his eyes, became troubled and contaminated and so was traded in (given up to social welfare) and cloned for another model (*Plays 4* 2008: 197–98).

The playtext

Written for two actors, *A Number* premiered at the Royal Court, was directed by Stephen Daldry, and starred Sir Michael Gambon as Salter and Daniel Craig as three of his sons, one biological (B1) and two clones (B2 and Michael Black). Craig has since confirmed that Churchill was 'present throughout rehearsals' and that 'she loves being there, in the thick of it, trying to make sense of it all'.[6] Cloning had been prominent in public discourse but, interestingly, Gambon revealed in an interview that Churchill was galvanised to write the play after a nightmare about her grandson, whom she dreamt had been abused (Gussow 2004: 123). A vision of a personal family horror, then, channelled her research into a sequence of searing scenes between a flawed, wretchedly duplicitous father and three of his sons.

In *A Number*, Churchill presents the emotional maelstrom caused by a hidden cloning experiment, which appears to have resulted in not one clone as intended by the DNA donor, Salter, but a batch. In scenes 1 and 3, B2, who has always been led to believe he was Salter's biological son, confronts him about the existence of 'a number' of clones. Salter is well-practised at evasion and denial, but B2's enquiries result in a slow leak of information, and Salter is forced to renege on each earlier lie and a sinister story emerges. B2 discovers that he is not the biological son, but one of 20 clones; that his mother was not his mother and was dead before he was born; that she was not killed in a car crash but committed suicide; and that Salter was a drunkard and singularly failed at fatherhood with his biological son, B1, inflicting serious damage and suffering on him before giving him up to social services at the age of four. B2's mental disintegration is swift: he feels a hatred for the 'father' he has hitherto loved but tries to rationalise Salter's treatment of B1 by arguing that his past alcoholism might be the result of a genetic legacy. B2 appreciates that he knew Salter as a good father but cannot reconcile himself to Salter's cruelty towards B1 and no longer knows how to relate to him: anxious to exonerate him, he also now knows he is guilty of appalling neglect. In addition, B2 has a horror of coming into contact with the other clones, and is terrified that B1, whom he regards as 'a nutter' and 'very something terrible' will kill him (*Plays 4* 2008: 187, 189), and flees in fear of his life: 'I don't feel myself and there's the others too, I don't want to see them I don't want them' (*Plays 4* 2008: 188).

In scene 2, B1 meets Salter for the first time since he was 'sent away' (*Plays 4* 2008: 177). B1 is enraged, violent and bordering on psychotic. His companions in life are not humans but dogs, and his treatment of them suggests a mirroring of Salter's treatment of him as a toddler: 'rottweiler pit bull I had to throw a chair, you could hit it with a belt it kept coming back' (*Plays 4* 2008: 180). B1 reveals to Salter that he lives in terror of him as a 'dark, dark power' (*Plays 4* 2008: 176), and presses him about his failure to respond to his repeated shouting for help night after night. Salter defends his decision to give B1 away and clone him, saying it was the best course of action because, paradoxically, he wanted the 'same perfect raw materials' (*Plays 4* 2008: 182). Churchill clearly constructs B1 as a victim of Salter's abuse and neglect: B1 is tortured by a persecution complex, consumed with rage at his usurper B2, and has no capacity to do anything other than objectify humans and animals, perceiving other living things as a lethal threat:

> Because this minute we sit here there's somebody a lot of them
> but think of one of them on the electric bedsprings or water

poured down his throat and jump on his stomach. There's a
lot of wicked people. So that's why. And you see them all
around you.

(Plays 4 2008: 181)

In scene 4, B1 returns to inform Salter that he followed B2 to his
hiding place and murdered him. Salter says that he blames himself,
that B1 should have killed him instead, offers to kill himself, and
perversely asks whether B1 has plans to annihilate the other clones,
which he says he would understand. In an extraordinarily chilling
monologue Salter reveals that he *did* hear B1 shouting as a child but
ignored him or went out, fed him food in the filth under his bed and
locked him in a cupboard, and that eventually B1 stopped eating
and speaking, and hid himself away. In a moment of uncontrolled
sadism, Salter actually congratulates himself on the virtue of not
killing B1:

> I could have killed you and I didn't I may have done terrible
> things but I didn't kill you. [...] I spared you though you were
> this disgusting thing by then anyone in their right mind would
> have squashed you but I remembered what you'd been like
> at the beginning and I spared you, I didn't want a different one,
> I wanted that again because you were perfect just like that and
> I loved you.

(Plays 4 2008: 197)

Salter's still festering subconscious desire to murder his biological
son finally has its effect, and we learn in scene 5 that B1 has since
committed suicide. Scenes 1 to 4 stand in contrast with the final
scene in which Salter meets a cloned son, Michael Black – cheerful,
full of light and love – who is thrilled to discover that he has cloned
brethren. Salter can find nothing of his own darkness or destructiveness in Michael, who is free of the resentment and chaos in him
that was present in B1 and B2. Apparently disappointed by
Michael's happiness and his own powerlessness over him, Salter
cannot relate to Michael and, critically, cannot re-find his two dead
sons in him. Michael sees Salter's failings for what they are and
does not judge him, but in the last lines of the play makes an ironic
apology to Salter for his autonomy:

SALTER: And you're happy you say are you? You like your life?
MICHAEL: I do yes, sorry.

(*Plays 4* 2008: 206)

Michael has a secure sense of identity and exerts an autonomy by virtue of an upbringing independent of Salter.

A Number and the zeitgeist

The plot of *A Number* allows Churchill to investigate fundamental questions about masculinity, the mystery of personal identity and to examine the widespread belief that there is a spiritual 'essence' unique to every individual. The questions posed by the play are as much existential as they are scientific. How do we understand our relation to other humans and ourselves? What do we think constitutes who we are and how do we characterise individuality? What is personality? How do we describe who we are? What role do biology and family history play in our sense of identity? How does family history and upbringing impact on us? How much do genes predetermine our lives? How do family members, in this case fathers and sons, define themselves in relation to each other? As the psychoanalyst Adam Phillips has argued: 'Cloning is for obvious, and not so obvious reasons, a compelling way of talking about what goes on between people' (Phillips 1998: 94). Churchill uses it to explore a family catastrophe on the scale of a Greek tragedy, involving neglect and abandonment, mental breakdown, denial, guilt, fratricide and suicide:

> *A Number* has cloning at the centre of its story but I never quite feel it's a play about cloning [...] – it lets me look at a lot of the things that interest me. I realised after I'd written it that I'd thought about some of the same things in *Identical Twins* more than twenty-five years earlier.
>
> (*Plays 4* 2008: viii)

It is clear from Churchill's plot structure and her character blueprints that she believes environment and parental influence have powerful effects on the health and stability of offspring. Salter's abuse of B1 and his denial of culpability infect his relationship with B2.

Churchill's collapsing of new genetics into contemporary existential angst, staged in a series of elliptical encounters, and written
mostly in sparse, incomplete sentences, haunted audiences. For
John Peter of the *Sunday Times*, *A Number* confirmed Churchill's
status as the first dramatist of the twenty-first century: 'it postulates
a social and spiritual existence that is both rigidly controlled and
uncontrollable: a quintessential 21st-century condition. [...] This
century is at a crossroads where metaphysical speculation meets
genetic possibilities, psychological puzzles and moral challenges.'[7]
Critics were struck by the juxtaposition of the ferocious emotional
intensity generated by the actors and the 'weirdly stylised', everyday
inarticulacies in Churchill's dialogue; by the 'dreamlike' twists and
'teasing' unfolding of the father's lies to B2 and his callous abandonment of his biological son, B1; and by the spiralling sense of
danger as the sons begin to unravel.[8] For Charles Spencer, not
famed for his enthusiasm for the experimental, *A Number* was 'one
of the most spellbinding and challenging theatrical events of the
year', and combined 'elegant structural simplicity with an astonishing intellectual and emotional depth'.[9] Superlatives have greeted
productions of *A Number* in many countries and America was no
exception. For Ben Brantley of the *New York Times*, Churchill's
play drew a portrait 'that portends a scary, brave new family for
which the rules have yet to be written'. It did no less than 'ponder a
threat to the very cornerstone of Western civilisation since the
Renaissance: the idea of human individuality, a subject Churchill
manages to probe in depth in a mere hour of spartan sentences and
silences. It is hard to think of another contemporary playwright
who combines such economy of means and breadth of imagination.'[10] Within a decade, *A Number* has become a staple of university drama curricula and now ranks with *Top Girls* as
Churchill's most celebrated play.

A Number: the Royal Court premiere and international interpretations

This section examines material from: the premiere starring Daniel
Craig and Michael Gambon; the 2004 production in America featur-
ing Sam Shepard and Dallas Roberts at the New York Theater
Workshop; and the Australian premiere at The Space Theatre in

Adelaide in 2004, in which Frank Gallacher played Salter and Marcus Graham played his sons. These productions are framed against the performance of *A Number* by an actual father and son, Timothy and Samuel West, at the Sheffield Crucible Theatre in 2006.

In conversation with Mel Gussow, who has acknowledged that *A Number* is 'one of Churchill's most disturbing and penetrating plays' (Gussow 2004: 122), Gambon has let it be known that he found the elliptical nature of Churchill's text a challenge from his first reading of it, and that rehearsals were painstaking and complex. Churchill did not offer psychological transparency for her characters nor seek to explain motivation, but preferred to see what intellectual and emotional discoveries the actors made for themselves (Gussow 2004: 123). To a reader, Salter is at once a titanic and terrible figure, manipulative, brutal and at moments psychopathic, as well as wounded, guilt-wracked, frail and pathetic. Confronted by his lies, it is never clear how many more untruths he may still be concealing, and the precise nature of his abuse and depth of his capacity for violence rumble up through the play in subterranean quakes. We never know to what extent Salter consciously or unconsciously aided and abetted his wife's suicide and whether he was the cause of her unhappiness. In his mind she has been strangely deleted, just as B1 was rejected and expelled. On the surface, Churchill's text is deceptively simple but actors are agreed that its underlying seismic shifts are taxing and require deep internal work. Despite all his expertise and experience 'the Great Gambon'[11] found *A Number* 'too difficult and too intense to do for a longer run' (Gussow 2004: 123). The details of the different sides of Salter's personality came to him gradually:

> I found that after we opened I made quite big changes in my approach to it. For the first week or so, I was a bit flat, I think. I didn't give enough variation with each son, in each of the five scenes. So after a few weeks I found myself playing that man sort of very different in each scene.
>
> (Gussow 2004: 129)

Much time in rehearsal was spent puzzling out potential meanings offered by stressing words differently, and considering Salter's dissemblances to his three sons. An actor who likes to make discoveries through his body, and to physicalise the internal (Gussow 2004: 130), Gambon found that small gestures, such as touching Daniel Craig's face, were tender and moving, and moments of falling to his knees or collapsing to the floor were highly charged. He was particularly interested in trying to capture something of Salter's duality, and in a moment that the critics found especially effective, and which Gussow described as 'an artfully contradictory picture of a man torn between compassion [...] and callousness', collapsed on the floor in tears, letting spirals of cigarette smoke rise above him (Gussow 2004: 122). For Gambon, the rehearsals were about trying to discover moments of eruption: 'The sections where there are big breakdowns and collapsing on stage, and screaming, that's nowhere in the text. You can find an indication of it in the stress in the words' (Gussow 2004: 129). Universally praised, Gambon's performance elicited completely different responses from critics, Michael Billington defining his portrayal as 'by turns explosively angry and wearily remorseful' and John Peter asserting that it was 'one of the most subtle and compelling performances of Gambon's career'.[12]

Craig's challenge was to find the physical differentiation between the three sons, with no opportunity to change costume. Throughout Craig wore a white T-shirt and jeans, but found a physicality through B2's increasing anxiety and confusion, his gradual drawing back from Salter, and his politeness and courtesy. Craig found a restless belligerence in B1, a constant watchfulness and hostility, sudden menacing movements, a tensing of fists and an aggressively set jaw. For Michael, his stance was relaxed and at ease, and denoted a curiosity and generosity in his interaction with others.[13] The celebrated voice coach Patsy Rodenburg helped Craig to map a difference through accent: B2 spoke a received English that suggested he was middle-class; B1 spoke with a cockney accent hinting at a rougher, working-class upbringing; and Michael had a soft, northwest accent and suggested his middle-class background through his profession as a teacher, his reading habits and his articulacy. Currently known for his interpretation of James Bond, Craig's performance in *A Number* relied on a set of different skills, namely meticulously constructed nuances. John Peter summed up the overwhelming critical reaction, calling it a 'virtuoso performance, precisely because it is so technically muted and unostentatious'.[14]

Ian MacNeil's unrelentingly empty space set composed of a wooden floor and just two chairs dwarfed the actors and highlighted the power struggle in each encounter. Next to Gambon's crumpled, besuited Salter with his lived-in, battered face and bear-like physicality, Craig's slight, youthful frame and his more elastic movement emphasised the differences between father and sons. The lack of resemblance between the two actors seemed to heighten a sense of Salter's increasing monstrousness, narcissism and isolation.

A Number in New York

In 2004 Sam Shepard was enticed back to New York theatre by the part of Salter after a 30-year absence. One of America's greatest experimental playwrights and a distinguished actor, Shepard's commitment to *A Number* attracted substantial press attention, as did Dallas Roberts' agreement to play opposite him, having made a name for himself in Lanford Wilson's play *Burn This* and the film *A Home at the End of the World*. Directed by James Macdonald of the Royal Court at the New York Theater Workshop, this interpretation intensified the idea of scientific experiment and the Chinese box effect of the shifting positions and perspectives created through Salter's tissue of lies and revelations. The designer, Eugene Lee, rebuilt the stage interior to simulate a nineteenth-century anatomy theatre, the audience seated on a steep rake looking down into a space lit up by a harsh glare. It was, in Brantley's words, a playing space, 'suitable for the performance of autopsies' and 'appropriate for a play that anatomises the impact of a scientific pursuit' but he warned that clinical detachment was exploded by the primal power of the confrontation between a father and his sons.[15] Shepard performed Salter as at the end of his game and his powers: dark, culpable, but none the less tragic, and still capable of wresting pity from others. For Brantley and others, Shepard, a writer who has specialised in personal and social disintegration from his own viewpoint, proved to be 'an ideal interpreter' of Churchill's elliptical play, words flowing from his mouth 'like blood from an open vein'.[16] Shepard found the impetus for tragedy in Salter's statements that the clone B2 provided him with an opportunity to right a wrong, to have a second chance in life:

I did try that's what I did I started again [...] I was good I tried to be good [...] I didn't feel I'd lost him when I sent him away because I had the second chance. And when my second one my son the second son was murdered it wasn't so bad as you'd think because it seemed fair.

(Plays 4 2008: 193, 205)

Shepard was as interested in Salter's masochism and self-destructiveness as he was in his sadism. A quieter interpretation than Gambon's, but equally intense, Shepard concentrated on what had been hollowed out and numbed or killed off in Salter through his alcoholism, his wife's death and his neglect and torture of B1. As Shepard saw it:

He's dealing with a terrible, terrible mistake he tries to correct, and in trying to correct it he created an even worse disaster. On the surface, he deals with anger, arrogance, denial. But underneath he's haunted by guilt and remorse. Underneath the language is this tremendous emotional base that you have to be vulnerable to. You have to listen very closely. You have to follow the veins and the rivers and the creeks and everything the language is leading you to. Every once in a while, it just erupts.

(Roberts 2008: 153)

Shepard's interpretation of Salter focused on a character whose energies are largely spent; his fire has all but burnt out though embers flicker and occasionally burst into flame. The combustibility and explosiveness Shepard found had shades of Gambon's more vehement portrayal. Dallas Roberts' incarnations of the sons, on the other hand, slid into each other as interrelated versions of the same negative and explored a link to Salter's slyness and duplicity, suggesting – unlike Craig's renderings (and Churchill's portrait of Michael) – that genes and biology outweigh environmental factors in the formation of personality. This effect was heightened by a plausible physical resemblance between Roberts and Shepard in terms of facial pallor, hair colour and build, and by similar hues in their costumes.[17] Roberts's interpretations played into Macintosh's nightmarish mythologies of identity fallacy and there were moments when his version of each son was as eerie and unsettling as the creation of Salter.

A *Number* in Australia

Frank Gallacher and Marcus Graham, who appeared in the Australian premiere directed by Marion Potts in 2004, likened Salter to King Lear. Gallacher found the encounter with three sons, as opposed to three daughters, and a father grappling with rage, guilt and self-fragmentation 'terrifyingly close', and reminiscent of the emotional scale of Shakespeare's play.[18] For Graham, as the sons, *A Number* was about 'human nature and what makes a person who they are. We have ninety-nine per cent the same genes, so it's only that one per cent that determines the difference.'[19] Like Craig, Graham saw the sons as quite different from one another, although genetically identical, and concentrated on where they had grown up, what their education was and what sort of environmental stresses they had known: his visual analogy for Churchill's play was the fascination with infinity and multidimensionality evident in an Escher drawing 'where the stairs never end.'[20] Gallacher's and Graham's visual imagining of Churchill's creation of multiple perspectives was strikingly developed in comparison to the actors in the English and American productions, possibly because framing was a literal feature of the director's and designer's concept. A large lopsided picture-frame captured an image of a bed, mattress and sheets that morphed into a pristine, abstracted landscape, suggesting the transformation of sex and conception into a digitally enhanced world of endless copies.[21] Intrigued by the perspectival shifts in *A Number*, Gallacher compared its detailed structures to the sculptural complexity contained within a magnetic resonance image or to the project of cubist art:

> Churchill uses cloning to circumnavigate father-son relationships, exploring three scenarios, so you get the three-dimensional picture. It's a cubist's appreciation of cloning, and a structure that allows for changing viewpoints.[22]

Familial hauntings: *A Number* at the Sheffield Crucible

Samuel West programmed *A Number* into the Sheffield Crucible repertoire in 2006 while he was artistic director, and at the time spoke of his reverence for Churchill's skill:

I think Churchill is consistently the most experimental dramatist in Britain. I firmly believe *A Number* is the best play I've read this century. You never know where she's going next and that unpredictability of form and content makes her a very unusual playwright. I think her plays offer a content in search of a form.[23]

However, for Samuel West (SW) the production of *A Number* was unthinkable without the casting of two actors who not only resembled each other but were actually father and son. His father, Timothy West (TW), was of the same view, as they revealed in a question and answer session with an audience after one of their performances.

SW: I wouldn't have done this play if my father hadn't been available. The play makes so much sense when cast this way that I actually couldn't conceive of it otherwise. We look like one another and that really adds all sorts of layers of meaning to the play.

TW: In the premiere Daniel Craig did not resemble Michael Gambon and that was a missed opportunity.[24]

As a member of the audience on different nights, I can confirm that the unmistakable family likeness between the actors, and the sense of occasion of watching two celebrated performers both playing at and being father and son, had extraordinary resonances, and at times cut through the fiction of the art in disturbing ways. Depending on the mood of the night, audiences either laughed or tensed up on certain exchanges – one exchange between Salter and B2 seemed particularly dangerous:

SALTER: just wait, because I'm your father.
B2:   You know that?
SALTER: of course.
B2:   It was all normal, everything, birth.
SALTER: you think I wouldn't know if I wasn't your father?

(*Plays 4* 2008: 166–67)

On stage the family likeness had an uncanny effect and the boundaries between the private world of the father and son and their

Figure 8.1 Timothy West in *A Number*, Sheffield Crucible © Manuel Harlan

celebrated status as professional actors became radically blurred with the dramatic narratives of Salter and his sons. I found myself wondering to what degree the Wests were drawing on their actual relationship with each other, and on their shared understanding of the process of acting. I also found myself pondering that although Churchill's fictional mother in *A Number* is dead, Timothy West's wife and Samuel West's mother, Prunella Scales, was very much alive and also a well-known and respected actress. The questions from the audience reflected similar preoccupations: there was a frisson in the auditorium when one spectator asked Samuel West if he thought acting was in his genes:

I'm the fourth generation of actors in my family but I don't think acting is in the blood. We've been interviewed a lot for this production and journalists have a way of referring to the West dynasty. I don't like that word. Among ourselves we refer to acting as 'the family business'. Acting wasn't inevitable for me.[25]

It is interesting, and not surprising, that Samuel West emphasised the impact of environment and the learned craft of acting, elements that highlighted a desire to separate himself from the question of genetic inheritance. His physical resemblance to Timothy West

Figure 8.2 Timothy and Samuel West in *A Number*, Sheffield Crucible
© Manuel Harlan

encouraged a presumption of psychological similarity and shared method of acting which Samuel West took pains to counter: his way of working was by 'a Stanislavskian language of actioning', he explained, and his father's through 'suggestion and discussion'.[26]

The text itself presented the same challenges to the Wests as it had to actors in the other productions, but they, like Gambon and Craig, had the advantage of Churchill's personal involvement. Intriguingly, the Wests seem to have been more alert to the rhythms and repetitions of words and phrases between B2 and Salter – and, indeed, echo each other in real life as is apparent below:

TW: We really had to work at the overlapping dialogue.
SW: It's difficult to commit to memory.
TW: If you decide to inflect a word a certain way, you manifestly change the meaning of the whole of the next page, so rehearsals were careful explorations of possible meanings. It's meticulously written. The echoes in the text are interesting: the character B2, for example, has picked up some of his father's rhythms.
SW: Caryl was extremely exact about how she meant the text to be interpreted.[27]

The Wests also gave themselves a more concrete narrative for Salter's abuse of B1 and a more detailed reason for why B1 might perceive his father as a 'dark, dark power'. They deduced that their relationship 'hid a horror' of sexual abuse that was suggested in the line: 'Things that are what I did that are not trivial like banana icecream nor unifuckingversal like turning over in bed' (*Plays 4* 2008: 205).[28]

This added 'horror' certainly provides another rationale for Salter's extreme reaction to B1, his evasion and denial, his compulsion to cast him away, as well as his wife's depression and suicide. It also makes sense of Salter's pathological mendacity and obliquity of vision. One wonders if Timothy and Samuel West, as a loving father and son, had to search harder for a reason that a father might mistreat and abandon his son.

At the Sheffield Crucible the Wests played in-the-round, which offered its own opportunities for experimenting with Churchill's multi-perspectival structure. The director took a decision that he would exploit the fall of light – experienced differently from each

Figure 8.3 Timothy and Samuel West in *A Number*, Sheffield Crucible
© Manuel Harlan

seat in the auditorium – to suggest the shifting surfaces and depths
in the characters and the narratives. Consequently, the lighting
designer, Hartley T.A. Kemp, was given a highly complex artistic
task that resulted in '149 lighting cues in a 49 minute play'.[29]

Lastly, Samuel West spoke of the challenge of creating a plausible
character for Michael. This may seem surprising given the relative
straightforwardness of Michael's encounter with Salter, but Michael
speaks little of himself and loves by deed. Understandably, Michael
struggles to describe himself to a man he has never met. History
will not repeat, apparently a blow to Salter who is unmoored by

Michael's separateness. Other actors have also battled with portraying Michael and in her latest introduction to the play Churchill gives a rare character direction:

> I'm reluctant to give advice [...] but I will point out that Michael isn't a fool. It's easy to make him a laughing stock to the audience, because he fails to come up with something that satisfies Salter, but his answers seem to me good ones and a serious answer to Salter's search for some essence of a person. That doesn't mean there aren't laughs in the scene
>
> (*Plays 4* 2008: viii).

In a poignant last exchange, the Wests mused on what it might mean to suffer the death of a child and Samuel West revealed his inclination to believe the resurrection fallacy. Interestingly, his father did not:

SW: In rehearsal the most difficult speech for me was Michael's speech about his wife's ears. I love the way Churchill has written his character. [...] Michael Black talks of the things and people he loves – his wife and children are part of him. He's been loved enough to devote himself to his family. He's the product of the love that's been shown to him. How do any of us talk about ourselves? What is it that gives us an identity? It's the details, the idiosyncrasies. Churchill is saying something about the very intangibility of identity, the difficulty in describing who we are.

TW: Salter could well be looking for a replica of the sons he's lost but Michael Black is himself. He isn't an emotional copy – that's the point, cloning is about physicality not psychology.

SW: If a child dies what parent would not want to bring that child back? And the idea of cloning yourself is intriguing.

TW: You can't recreate in your own image. You'd always be disappointed, always be looking for elements which are absent. And of course how we perceive ourselves is not how others perceive us.[30]

Fascinatingly, even in the question and answer session, at different moments the Wests appealed to each other sometimes as father and son, sometimes as friends, sometimes as professional actors, and sometimes as artistic director and employee. The brilliance of the casting idea rendered the puzzle of this play even more mysterious and multilayered. Uncannily, at certain instances in performing *A Number*, the Wests' familial resemblance and real-life connection shot down the creation of theatrical illusion.

Notes

1 See Meredith Wadman, 'Cloning Special: Dolly: A Decade On', *Nature* 445(7130), 22 February 2007: 800–1.
2 See Barbara MacKinnon (ed.), *Human Cloning: Science, Ethics and Public Policy* (Urbana: University of Illinois Press, 2002); B.R. Sharma, 'Cloning Controversies: An Overview of the Science, Ethics and Politics', *Medicine, Science and the Law*,45(1), January 2005: 17–26; and Arlene Klotzko (ed.), *The Cloning Sourcebook* (Oxford: Oxford University Press, 2001).
3 One problem with regulation, especially in America, is that privately funded institutions have greater autonomy in their research programmes.
4 Lee M. Silver, 'What Are Clones? They're Not What You Think They Are', *Nature* 21, 2001: 412.
5 See also Amit Marcus, 'The Ethics of Human Cloning in Narrative Fiction', *Comparative Literature Studies*, 49(3), 2012: 405–33.
6 Interview by Lucy Powell, *The Times*, 1 September 2008.
7 John Peter, *Sunday Times*, 6 October 2002. Nicholas de Jongh described *A Number* as 'the first true play of the 21st century', *Evening Standard*, 27 September 2002.
8 Benedict Nightingale, *The Times*, 29 September 2002; Kate Bassett, *Independent on Sunday*, 29 September 2002; John Peter, *Sunday Times*, 6 October 2002.
9 Charles Spencer, *Daily Telegraph*, 27 September 2002.
10 Ben Brantley, *New York Times*, 8 December 2004.
11 Actor Ralph Richardson's popular coinage, *The London Gazette*, 29 December 1989.
12 Michael Billington, *The Guardian*, 27 September 2002; John Peter, *Sunday Times*, 6 October 2002.
13 Author's notes from seeing production.
14 John Peter, *Sunday Times*, 6 October 2002.
15 Ben Brantley, *New York Times*, 8 December 2004.
16 Ben Brantley, *New York Times*, 8 December 2004.
17 Author's notes from seeing production.
18 Patrick McDonald, *Adelaide Advertiser*, 26 April 2004. See also Matt Byrne, *Sunday Mail*, 2 May 2004.
19 Patrick McDonald, *Adelaide Advertiser*, 26 April 2004.

20 Patrick McDonald, *Adelaide Advertiser*, 26 April 2004.
21 Tim Lloyd, *Adelaide Advertiser*, 15 May 2004.
22 Patrick McDonald, *Adelaide Advertiser*, 26 April 2004.
23 Question and answer session with Sheffield Crucible audience, 9 November 2006, Sheffield Crucible Archive.
24 Samuel and Timothy West, Q&A, 9 November 2006.
25 Samuel West, Q&A, 9 November 2006.
26 Samuel West, Q&A, 9 November 2006.
27 Samuel and Timothy West, Q&A, 9 November 2006.
28 Samuel and Timothy West, Q&A, 9 November 2006.
29 Samuel and Timothy West, Q&A, 9 November 2006.
30 Samuel and Timothy West, Q&A, 9 November 2006.

9 Afterword

Children, carnage and the human-supernatural

Sontag has argued that the founding idea of the critique of modernity is that 'life consists of a diet of horrors by which we are corrupted and to which we gradually become habituated' (Sontag 2003: 106). Churchill's life's work has sought to interrogate spectatorial operations of seeing in order to make visible the failings of authoritarian regimes and, in particular, capitalist socio-economics. Her latest experiments have continued to explore war, violence, globalisation and the effects of advanced communications technology. In *Drunk Enough to Say I Love You* (2006), Churchill provided a surreal map of the deadly history of America's post-Second World War foreign policy through the relationship between two men, Sam and Guy. Sam, as Churchill has explained, stands in for America, 'Uncle Sam, as in the political cartoon', and Guy for a man from whichever country the play is being performed in – although at the premiere Guy was read as indicative of Britain's so-called special relationship with the United States and many critics read the characters as George Bush and Tony Blair (*Plays 4* 2008: ix). Prompted by the Iraq War of 2003 and the American and British invasion of Iraq, yet another act of aggression (some would say a war crime) that America justified as necessary for world 'peace' and 'security',[1] *Drunk Enough* alludes to America's litany of attacks on other countries since 1939, referencing bombings, interference in democratic elections, assassinations of political leaders, and attempts to suppress populist or nationalist movements. Sam and Guy show not the slightest empathy for the lives lost, relishing their political dominance, and their alienation to events and victims mirrored in the Royal Court production by the fact that the entire play took place on a sofa suspended high above the stage. Rachel Clements has persuasively argued that *Drunk Enough* is a new form of history play and that it is much illuminated by Judith Butler's theory of precarity, as it distorts and breaks the frames customarily developed around American foreign policy and exposes atrocity and mass killing (Clements 2014).

With *Seven Jewish Children: A Play for Gaza* (2009) Churchill responded directly to Israel's Operation Cast Lead, an offensive launched against Gaza in December 2008 that caused more than 1,400 Palestinian deaths, wounded 5,000 and destroyed thousands of homes. Composed of just seven scenes, the play appears to be a compacted history of the foundation of modern Israel after World War II. Its dissemination has been electronic and the play may only be produced if admission is free and donations for Medical Aid in Palestine collected. Thus the production of the play itself becomes an act of political and human rights intervention. Churchill's pro-Palestine politics caused widespread outrage among Zionists and the play provoked accusations of anti-Semitism.[2] Throughout the seven scenes, different groups of people rehearse what to tell an unseen girl about the conflict and killings. The seven girls remain absent but at the same the obsessive focus of the discussions. The girls' simultaneous abduction from and yet imprisonment within by the domestic by members of their own community is represented as a protective measure for their safety and the future survival of the state of Israel but is slowly revealed to be an uncanny act of aggression – the absent enemy and their children are doubled by the colonization and erasure of these spectral girls. Churchill's gender political preoccupations resurface but, disturbingly, the counter-narrative, the 'Other', is not permitted expression and is hidden from view. Even the ghosts, witches and undead women we have seen in past plays have disappeared – censorship is now total.

Churchill's most recent plays *Love and Information* (2012) and *Ding Dong the Wicked* (2012) suggest the increasing anatomisation of human life, and the loss of compassion and connection brought about by excess consumption, and the normalisation of war and extreme violence. In *Love and Information*, Churchill explores the global overload of information generated by social media networks and the internet. The horror of the human clone in *A Number* has been replaced with the disturbing passion for a virtual identity on Facebook and the greater desire for interface with technology than with another human. In a scene called 'Remote' a location without internet or mobile reception is presented as uncanny and intolerable because the individual only feels alive if she has electronic connectivity (*Love and Information* 2012: 13). Similarly, catastrophe is absorbed as a virtual entertainment and witnesses have no empathy with victims of calamity; speaking of an earthquake, a character reports: 'that black wave with the cars was awesome' (*Love and Information* 2012: 60). Wars are justified on the basis of manufactured information (an allusion to the supposed weapons of mass destruction in Iraq) and communications networks colonised by politicians.

The striking repeat trope in *Love and Information* is the child without fundamental human attributes. In the scene 'The Child Who Didn't Know Fear', a child attempts to learn what it might be to experience fear – but even gruesome encounters with the headless undead and monsters have no effect. S/he is eventually eaten by a lion because s/he has no understanding of risk. The 'Child Who Didn't Know Sorry' experiences no regret and does not comprehend why s/he is abnormal nor why expressions of regret for causing harm are morally reassuring. 'The Child Who Didn't Know Pain' presents a child who can suffer grotesque physical damage but feels no pain. Late capitalism, suggests Churchill, is breeding monster children on a grand scale and creating an apocalyptic future.

In *Ding Dong the Wicked* (2012) the trope of the imprisoned girl returns: two dysfunctional, violent families in different countries mirror one another by glorifying war and violence, neglecting and incarcerating the distressed young girl in their midst, proclaiming their sons war heroes and engaging in disturbing victory rituals at reports of enemy deaths. The girls are never seen but their misery is the subject of casual conversation and appears to be one reason that they cannot be integrated into the household. *Ding Dong the Wicked* is the title of the frenetic victory song by the Munchkins after the death of the Wicked Witch of the East in *The Wizard of Oz*. Life increasingly seems to imitate art, Churchill appears to be suggesting, and the trajectory of her artistic work currently leads to what I shall call her creation of the 'human-supernatural'. The Wicked Witch stands in for the newly created or perhaps long familiar enemies constructed throughout the Western world. Supernatural forces, Churchill's twenty-first-century plays increasingly imply, have ceased to be horrifying next to man-made evils, many beyond our understanding and perpetrated on an unfathomable scale every day. The radical evil of Sam and Guy in *Drunk Enough to Say I Love You* competes with and perhaps betters many monstrous supernatural villains. The callousness and extremity of human violence currently being exhibited in so many parts of the world now extends to supernatural proportions of its own. Hope and redemption are not to be found. Her current dramatic worlds heave with the psychic, emotional and physical destruction of children, suggesting that they are brought into the world only to be schooled and treated as a breed of the undead. Churchill's worlds of horror grow ever darker.

Notes

1 See for example, William Blum, *Rogue State* (New York: Common Courage 2005) and *America's Deadliest Export Democracy* (London: Zed Books, 2013); Noam Chomsky, *Hegemony or Survival: America's Quest for Global Dominance* (New York: Holt, 2004).
2 For example, Howard Jacobson, *The Independent*, 18 February 2009; Jonathan Romain, *The Guardian*, 20 February 2009; Dave Rich and Mark Gardner, *The Guardian*, 1 May 2009. See Churchill's response 'My Play is Not Anti-Semitic', *The Independent*, 21 February 2009.

Bibliography

Collections of plays

Plays 1 (1985) *Owners, Traps, Vinegar Tom, Light Shining in Buckinghamshire, Cloud Nine*, London: Methuen.

Plays 2 (1990) *Softcops, Top Girls, Fen, Serious Money*, London: Methuen.

Churchill Shorts: Short Plays by Caryl Churchill (1990) *Three More Sleepless Nights, Lovesick, The After-Dinner Joke, Abortive, Schreber's Nervous Illness, The Judge's Wife, The Hospital at the Time of the Revolution, Hot Fudge, Not Not Not Not Not Enough Oxygen, Seagulls*, London: Nick Hern Books.

Plays 3 (1998) *Icecream, Mad Forest, Thyestes, The Skriker, Lives of the Great Poisoners, A Mouthful of Birds*, London: Nick Hern Books.

Plays 4 (2008) *Hotel, This is a Chair, Blue Heart, Far Away, A Number, A Dream Play, Drunk Enough to Say I Love You?* London: Nick Hern Books.

Plays in other editions

The Ants (1969) in *New English Dramatists*, vol 12, Harmondsworth: Penguin.

Owners (1973), London: Methuen.

Cloud Nine (1979), London: Pluto Press.

Traps, (1979), London: Pluto Press. Subsequent edition (1989), London: Nick Hern Books.

Vinegar Tom (1982), in M. Wandor (ed.) *Plays By Women: Volume One*, London: Methuen.

Top Girls (1982) London: Methuen. Subsequent editions include (1990) Samuel French, Acting Edition; (1991) Methuen Student Edition; (2001) Methuen Modern Plays.

Fen (1983), London: Methuen.

Objections to Sex and Violence (1985), in M. Wandor (ed.) *Plays By Women: Volume Four*, London: Methuen.

Softcops and Fen (1986), London: Methuen.

A Mouthful of Birds (1986), London: Methuen.

Serious Money (1987), London: Methuen. Subsequent editions include (1990) Methuen Modern Plays; (1990) Samuel French, Acting Edition; (2002) Methuen Student Edition.

Icecream (1989), London: Nick Hern Books.

Mad Forest: A Play From Romania (1991), London: Nick Hern Books.

Lives of the Great Poisoners: A Production Dossier (1993), London: Methuen.

The Skriker (1994), London: Nick Hern Books.

Thyestes [Seneca] (trans.) (1995), London: Nick Hern Books.

The After-Dinner Joke and Three More Sleepless Nights (1995), Cambridge Literature Series, Cambridge: Cambridge University Press.

Light Shining in Buckinghamshire (1996), London: Nick Hern Books.

Blue Heart (1997), London: Nick Hern Books.

Hotel (1997), London: Nick Hern Books.

This is a Chair (1999), London: Nick Hern Books.

Far Away (2000), London: Nick Hern Books.

A Number (2002), London: Nick Hern Books.

A Dream Play (2005) [A. Strindberg] A new version, London: Nick Hern Books.

Drunk Enough to Say I Love You? (2006), London: Nick Hern Books.

Bliss. [Olivier Choinière] (trans) (2008), London: Nick Hern Books.

Seven Jewish Children (2009), London: Nick Hern Books, www.nickhern books.co.uk/Book/279/Seven-Jewish-Children.html.

Love and Information (2012), London: Nick Hern Books.

Ding Dong the Wicked (2012), London: Nick Hern Books.

Essays

Churchill, Caryl (1960) 'Not Ordinary, Not Safe: A Direction for Drama?', *The Twentieth Century*, 168(1005): 443–51.

Interviews

Armitstead, C. (1994) 'Tale of the Unexpected', *The Guardian*, 12 January.

Benedict, D. (1997) 'The Mother of Reinvention', *The Independent*, 19 April.

Betsko, K. and Koenig, R. (eds.) (1987) 'Caryl Churchill', *Interviews with Contemporary Women Playwrights*, New York: Beech Tree Books.

Cousin, G. (1988) 'The Common Imagination and the Individual Voice', *New Theatre Quarterly*,13: 1–16.

Gooch, S. (1973) 'Caryl Churchill', *Plays and Players*, January.

Gussow, M. (1987) 'Caryl Churchill: A Genteel Playwright with an Angry Voice', *New York Times*, 22 November.

Hayman, R. (1980) 'Partners: Caryl Churchill and Max Stafford-Clark', *Sunday Times Magazine*, 2 March.

Hiley, J. (1990) 'Revolution in Miniature', *The Times*, 10 October.

Jackson, K. (1989) 'Incompatible Flavours', *The Independent*, 12 April.

Kay, J. (1989) 'Interview with Caryl Churchill', *New Statesman and Society*, 21 April.

Mackrell, J. (1994) 'Flights of Fancy', *The Independent*, 20 January.

McFerran, A. (1977) 'The Theatre's (Somewhat) Angry Young Women', *Time Out*, 28 October.

Robinson, M. (1991) 'Bracing Grace: Wing-Davey's "Front-Foot" Approach to *Mad Forest*', *Village Voice*, 24 December.

Simon, J. (1983) 'Sex, Politics, and Other Play Things', *Vogue*, August.

Thomas, C. (1990) 'Not out of the Wood', *Plays and Players*, August.

Thurman, J. (1982) 'The Playwright Who Makes you Laugh about Orgasm, Racism, Class Struggle, Homophobia, Woman-Hating, the British Empire, and the Irrepressible Strangeness of the Human Heart', *Ms*, May.

Truss, L. (1984) 'A Fair Cop', *Plays and Players*, January.

Vidal, J. (1986) 'Legend of a Woman Possessed', *The Guardian*, 21 November.

Winner, L. (1990) 'Caryl Churchill, Ex-Ideologue, Trusts to Luck', *New York Times*, 29 April.

Books, essays and articles on Caryl Churchill

Adiseshiah, S. (2009) *Churchill's Socialism: Political Resistance in the Plays of Caryl Churchill*, Newcastle: Cambridge Scholars.

Amich, C. (2007) 'Bringing the Global Home: The Commitment of Caryl Churchill's *The Skriker*', *Modern Drama* 50(3): 394–413.

Amoko, A. (1999) 'Casting Aside Colonial Occupation: Intersections of Race, Sex and Gender in *Cloud Nine* and *Cloud Nine* Criticism', *Modern Drama*, 42(1): 45–54.

Aston, E. (2001) *Caryl Churchill*, second edition, Tavistock: Northcote House.

——(2003) *Feminist Views on the English Stage*, Cambridge: Cambridge University Press.

——(2005) '"A Licence to Kill": Caryl Churchill's Socialist-Feminist "Ideas of Nature"', in G. Giannachi and N. Stewart (eds.), *Performing Nature: Explorations in Ecology and the Arts*, Bern: Peter Lang.

Aston, E. and Case, S.E. (eds.) (2007) *Staging International Feminisms*, Basingstoke: Palgrave.

Aston, E. and Diamond, E. (eds.) (2009) *Cambridge Companion to Caryl Churchill*, Cambridge: Cambridge University Press.

Bazin, V. (2006) '"[Not] Talking 'Bout My Generation": Historicizing Feminisms in Caryl Churchill's *Top Girls*', *Studies in the Literary Imagination*, 39(2): 115–34.

Bloom, M. (1990) 'International Flavours Spice Churchill's Works', *American Theatre*, November: 60–70.

Brewer, M. (2005) 'Colonial Metaphors of Blackness and the Reality of White Racial Oppression: Caryl Churchill's *Cloud Nine*', in *Staging Whiteness*, Connecticut: Wesleyan University Press.

Burke, J.T. (1993) '*Top Girls* and the Politics of Representation', in E. Donkin and S. Clement (eds.), *Upstaging Big Daddy: Directing Theater as if Gender and Race Matter*, Ann Arbor: University of Michigan Press.

Clements, R. (2013) 'Framing War, Staging Precarity: Caryl Churchill's *Seven Jewish Children* and the Spectres of Vulnerability', *Contemporary Theatre Review*, 23(3): 357–67.

——(2014) 'Apprehending the Spectral: Hauntology and Precarity in Caryl Churchill's Plays', in M. Luckhurst and E. Morin (eds.), *Theatre and Ghosts: Materiality, Performance, Modernity*, London: Palgrave.

Cousin, G. (1989) *Churchill the Playwright*, London: Methuen.

Diamond, E. (1985) 'Refusing the Romanticism of Identity: Narrative Interventions in Churchill, Benmussa, Duras', *Theatre Journal*, 37(3): 273–86.

——(1988) '(In)Visible Bodies in Churchill's Theatre', *Theatre Journal*, 40(2): 188–204.

——(2006) 'Caryl Churchill: Feeling Global', in M. Luckhurst (ed.) *A Companion to Modern British and Irish Drama 1880–2005*, Oxford: Blackwell.

Doty, G. and Harbin, B. (1990) *Inside the Royal Court 1956–81*, Louisiana: Louisiana State University Press.

Dymkowski, C. (2003) 'Caryl Churchill: Far Away … but Close to Home', *European Journal of English Studies*, 7(1): 55–68.

Edwardes, J. (2006) 'Celebrating Caryl Churchill', with A. de Angelis, S. Feehily and L. Wade, *Time Out*, 14 November.

Evan, R. (2002) 'Women and Violence in *A Mouthful of Birds*', *Theatre Journal*, 54(2): 263–84.

Fitzsimmons, L. (1987) 'I Won't Turn Back for You or Anyone: Caryl Churchill's Socialist-Feminist Theatre', *Essays in Theatre*, 6(1): 19–29.

——(1989) *File on Churchill*, London: Methuen.

Gardner, J. (1999) 'Caryl Churchill's *Top Girls*: Defining and Reclaiming Feminism in Thatcher's Britain', *New England Theatre Journal*, 10: 89–110.

Gobert, R. Darren (2014) *The Theatre of Caryl Churchill*, London: Methuen.

Gray, F. (1993) 'Mirrors of Utopia: Caryl Churchill and Joint Stock', in J. Acheson (ed.), *British and Irish Drama Since 1960*, Basingstoke: Macmillan.

Hammond, B.S. (2007) '"Is Everything History?" Churchill, Barker and the Modern History Play', *Comparative Drama*, 41(1): 1–23.

Hanna, G. (ed.) (1991) *Monstrous Regiment: A Collective Celebration*, London: Nick Hern Books.

Harding, J.M. (1998) 'Cloud Cover: (Re)Dressing Desire and Comfortable Subversions in Caryl Churchill's *Cloud Nine*', *PMLA*, 113(2): 258–72.

Innes, C. (1992) 'Caryl Churchill: Theatre as a Model for Change' *in Modern British Drama 1890–1990*, Cambridge: Cambridge University Press.

Itzin, C. (1980) 'Caryl Churchill', in *Stages in the Revolution: Political Theatre in Britain Since 1968*, London: Methuen: 279–87.

Jernigan, D. (2004) '*Traps, Softcops, Blue Heart* and *This is a Chair*: Tracking Epistemological Upheaval in Caryl Churchill's Shorter Plays', *Modern Drama*, 47(1): 21–43.

Keyssar, H. (1984) 'The Dramas of Caryl Churchill: the Politics of Possibility', in *Feminist Theatre*, Basingstoke: Macmillan.

Kintz, L. (1991) 'Performing Capital in Caryl Churchill's *Serious Money*', *Theatre Journal*, 51(3): 251–65.

Kritzer, A.H. (1991) *The Plays of Caryl Churchill: Theatre of Empowerment*, Basingstoke: Macmillan.

Lavell, I. (2002) 'Caryl Churchill's *The Hospital at the Time of the Revolution*', *Modern Drama*, 45(1): 76–94.

Marohl, J. (1987) 'De-realised Women: Performance and Identity in *Top Girls*', *Modern Drama*, 30(3): 376–88.

Martin, C. (ed.) (1996) *Sourcebook of Feminist Theatre*, London: Routledge.

Mitchell, T. (1993) 'Caryl Churchill's *Mad Forest*: Polyphonic Representations of Southeastern Europe', *Modern Drama*, 36(4): 499–511.

Neblett, R. (2003) '"Nobody Sings About It": In Defence of the Songs in Caryl Churchill's *Vinegar Tom*', *New England Theatre Journal*, 14: 101–22.

Pocock, S. (2007) '"God's in this Apple": Eating and Spirituality in Churchill's *Light Shining in Buckinghamshire*', *Modern Drama*, 50(1): 60–76.

Qian, J. (2011) 'Caryl Churchill in China', paper at Caryl Churchill Symposium, University of Lincoln, 16 April.

Rabillard, S. (1994) 'Churchill's *Fen* and the Production of a Feminist Ecotheatre', *Theater*, 25(1): 62–71.

——(ed.) (1998) *Essays on Caryl Churchill: Contemporary Representations*, Winnipeg: Blizzard Publishing.

Randall, P.R. (1988) *Caryl Churchill: A Casebook*, New York and London: Garland Publishing.

Ravenhill, M. (2008) 'She Made Us Raise Our Game', *The Guardian*, 3 September.

Reinelt, J. (1994) 'Caryl Churchill: Socialist Feminism and Brechtian Dramaturgy', in *After Brecht: British Epic Theater*, Ann Arbor: University of Michigan Press.

——(2000) 'Caryl Churchill and the Politics of Style' in E. Aston and J. Reinelt (eds.), *The Cambridge Companion to Modern British Women Playwrights*, Cambridge: Cambridge University Press.

Ritchie, R. (ed.) (1987) *The Joint Stock Book: The Making of a Theatre Collective*, London: Methuen.

Roberts, P. and Stafford-Clark, M. (2007) *Taking Stock: The Theatre of Max Stafford-Clark*, London: Nick Hern Books.

Roberts, P. (2008) *About Churchill: The Playwright and the Work*, London: Faber & Faber.

Sierz, A. (2011) *Rewriting the Nation: British Theatre Today*, London: Methuen.

Silverstein, M. (1994) '"Make Us the Women We Can't Be": *Cloud Nine* and the Female Imaginary', *Journal of Dramatic Theory and Criticism*, 8(2): 7–22.

Solomon, A. (1981) 'Witches, Ranters and the Middle Class: The Plays of Caryl Churchill', *Theater*, 12(2): 49–55.

Soto-Morettini, D. (1994) 'Revolution and the Fatally Clever Smile: Caryl Churchill's *Mad Forest*', *Journal of Dramatic Theory and Criticism*, 9(1): 105–18.

Spink, I. (1995) 'Collaborations', in *Border Tensions: Dance and Discourse, Proceedings of the Fifth Study of Dance Conference*, Surrey: Department of Dance Studies, University of Surrey: 293–302.

Swanson, M. (1986) 'Mother/Daughter Relationships, in Three Plays by Caryl Churchill', *Theatre Studies* 31: 49–66.

Thomas, J. (1992) 'The Plays of Caryl Churchill: Essays in Refusal', in A. Page (ed.), *The Death of the Playwright?* Basingstoke: Macmillan.

Tycer, A. (2008) *Caryl Churchill's* Top Girls, London and New York: Continuum.

Wandor, M. (1979) 'Free Collective Bargaining', *Time Out*, 30 March.

——(1987) 'Existential Women: *Owners* and *Top Girls*', in *Look Back in Gender: Sexuality and the Family in Post-War British Drama*, London: Methuen.

——. (2001) 'Biology and Property Values: *Owners*' and 'Utopias: *Cloud Nine*', in *Post-War British Drama: Looking Back in Gender*, London: Routledge.

Yan, H. (2002) 'Staging Modern Vagrancy: Female Figures of Border-crossing, in Ama Ata Aidoo and Caryl Churchill', *Theatre Journal*, 54(2): 245–62.

Web and media sources

Benedict, D. with Bassett, L., Cowley, G., Findlay, D. and Fisher, R. (2005) 'Reputations: Caryl Churchill', *Theatre Voice*, www.theatrevoice.com/the_archive.

Churchill, C. (1978) *The Legion Hall Bombing* (clips), BFI Screenonline, www.screenonline.org.uk/tv/id/557937.

——(1994) *The Skriker*, National Theatre Archive, London.

——(1994) Interview [*The Skriker*], Late Theatre, BBC2.

——. (1996), *Top Girls*, Approaching Literature Series [VHS video], Milton Keynes: Open University.

——. (2006), *We Turned on the Lights*, The Ashden Directory, www.ashden directory.org.uk.

Churchill, C. and Spink, I. (1988) *Fugue*, Channel 4, Dance-Lines.

Omnibus On Caryl Churchill (1988) BBC1.

Other works

Alexander, M.S., Evans, M. and Keiger, J.F.V. (eds.) (2002) *The Algerian War and the French Army*, London: Palgrave.

Alleg, H. (2006) *The Question*, New York: Bison Books.

Arendt, H. (1998) *The Banality of Evil*, London: Rowman and Littlefield.

Aston, E. and Harris, G. (eds.) (2006) *Feminist Futures? Theatre, Performance, Theory*, Cambridge: Cambridge University Press.

Aston, E. and Reinelt, J. (eds.) (2000) *The Cambridge Companion to Modern British Women Playwrights*, Cambridge: Cambridge University Press.

Bach, S. (2008) *Leni: The Life and Work of Leni Riefenstahl*, London: Vintage.

Barker, H. (1989) *Arguments for a Theatre*, London: John Calder.

Beech, M. and Lee, S. (2008) *Ten Years of New Labour*, London: Palgrave.

Behr, E. (1991) *The Rise and Fall of the Ceausescus*, London: Hamish Hamilton.

Billington, M. (2009) *The State of the Nation: British Theatre Since 1945*, London: Faber & Faber.

Bowins, B. (2010) 'Repetitive Maladaptive Behaviour: Beyond Repetition Compulsion', *The American Journal of Psychoanalysis*, 70: 282–98.

Brady, S. (2012) *Performance, Politics, and the War on Terror*, London: Palgrave.

Brailsford, H.L. (1961) *The Levellers and the English Revolution*, Stanford: Stanford University Press.

Brannigan, M.C. (2001) *Ethical Issues in Human Cloning*, New York and London: Seven Bridges.

Brecht, B. (1964) *Brecht on Theatre*, John Willett (trans.), London: Methuen.

Brière, J. (2004) *Psychological Assessment of Adult Post-traumatic States*, Washington, DC: American Psychological Association.

Butler, J. (1990a) *Gender Trouble: Feminism and the Subversion of Identity*, London and New York: Routledge.

——(1990b) 'Performative Acts and Gender Constitution: An Essay in Phenomenology and Feminist Theory', in S.-E. Case (ed.), *Performing Feminisms*, Baltimore: Johns Hopkins University Press.

——(2009) *Frames of War*, London: Verso.

Cantrell, T. (2013) *Acting in Documentary Theatre*, London: Palgrave.

Cantrell, T. and Luckhurst, M. (2010) *Playing for Real: Actors on Playing Real People*, London: Palgrave.

Case, S.-E. (1988) *Feminism and Theatre*, London: Routledge.

Chambers, C. (1997) *Peggy: The Life of Margaret Ramsay, Play Agent*, London: Nick Hern Books.

Climenhaga, R. (2009) *Pina Bausch*, London: Routledge.

Connelly, M. (2008) *A Diplomatic Revolution: Algeria's Fight for Independence and the Origins of the Cold War Era*, Oxford: Oxford University Press.

Deletant, D. (1995) *Ceausescu and the Securitate: Coercion and Dissent in Romania, 1965–1989*, London: Hurst and Co.

Deleuze, G. (1994) *Difference and Repetition*, London: Athlone Press.

Del Pilar Blanco, M. and Peeren, E. (eds.) (2013) *The Spectralities Reader*, London: Bloomsbury.

Derrida, J. (2006) *Specters of Marx*, London: Routledge.

Diamond, E. (1997) *Unmasking Mimesis: Essays on Feminism and Theater*, New York: Routledge.

Dromgoole, D. (2000) *The Full Room*, London: Methuen.

Ehrenreich, B. and English, D. (1973) *Witches, Midwives, and Nurses: A History of Women Healers*, New York: The Feminist Press.

Emanuel, K., Layzer, Judith A. and Mooman, William R. (2007) *What We Know about Climate Change*, Cambridge, MA: MIT Press.

Engel, J.A. (2009) *The Fall of the Berlin Wall: The Revolutionary Legacy of 1989*, Oxford: Oxford University Press.

Eyre, R. and Wright, N. (2000) *Changing Stages: A View of British Theatre in the Twentieth Century*, London: Bloomsbury.

Falk, B.J. (2003) *The Dilemmas of Dissidence in East-Central Europe*, Budapest: Buda.

Faludi, S. (1991) *Backlash*, London: Chatto & Windus.

Fanon, F. (1964) *Toward the African Revolution: Political Essays*, New York: Grove Press.

——(1967) *The Wretched of the Earth*, Harmondsworth: Penguin.

——(2008) *Black Skins, White Masks*, New York: Grove Press.

——(2011) *L'An de la Révolution Algérienne*, Paris: Decouverte.

Farfan, P. and Ferris, L. (eds.) (2013) *Contemporary Women Playwrights in the Twenty-First Century*, Basingstoke: Palgrave.

Figes, E. (1970) *Patriarchal Attitudes*, London: Persea Books.

Foucault, M. (1979) *Discipline and Punish: The Birth of the Prison*, London: Penguin.

Franklin, S. (2007) *Dolly Mixtures: The Remaking of Genealogy*, Durham, NC: Duke University Press.

Freud, S. (1955) *The Standard Edition of the Complete Psychological Works*, ed. J. Strachey, London: Hogarth Press.

Friedman, M. (1962) *Capitalism and Freedom*, Chicago: University of Chicago Press.

Gale, M.B. (2002) *West End Women: Women and the London Stage 1918–1962*, London: Routledge.

Gallagher, T. (1995) *Romania after Ceausescu*, Edinburgh: Edinburgh University Press.

Garton Ash, T. (2000) *History of the Present: Essays, Sketches and Dispatches from Europe in the 1990s*, London and New York: Random House.

Giannachi, G. and Luckhurst, M. (1999) *On Directing; Interviews with Directors*, London: Faber & Faber.

Gilberg, T. (1990) *Nationalism and Communism in Romania: The Rise and Fall of Ceausescu's Personal Dictatorship*, Boulder, CO: Westview Press.

Gleiser, K.A. (2008) 'Psychoanalytic Perspectives on Trauma Repetition', *Journal of Trauma and Dissociation*, 4(4): 27–47.

Glenny, M. (1990) *The Rebirth of History: Eastern Europe in the Age of Democracy*, London: Penguin.

——(2012) *The Balkans 1804–2012*, London: Granta.

Goldhagen, D. (1997) *Hitler's Willing Executioners: Ordinary Germans and the Holocaust*, London: Vintage.

Goodman, L. (1993) *Contemporary Feminist Theatres*, London: Routledge.

Greer, G. (1991) *Women, Ageing and the Menopause*, London: Ballantine.

Gussow, M. (2004) *Michael Gambon: A Life in Acting*, London: Nick Hern.

Hall, S. and Jacques, M. (eds.) (1983) *The Politics of Thatcherism*, London: Lawrence and Wishart.

Hill, C. (1991) *The World Turned Upside Down: Radical Ideas during the English Revolution*, London: Penguin.

Hoggan, J. and Littlemore, R. (2009) *Climate Cover-Up: The Crusade to Deny Global Warming*, London: Greystone.

Holdsworth, N. and Luckhurst, M. (eds.) (2008) *Contemporary British and Irish Drama*, Oxford: Blackwell.

Horne, A. (2006) *A Savage War of Peace: Algeria 1954–1962*, New York: New York Review of Books.

Hughes, J. (2011) *Performance in a Time of Terror*, Manchester: Manchester University Press.

Innes, C. (2002) *Modern British Drama*, Cambridge: Cambridge University Press.

Kershaw, B. (ed.) (2004) *British Theatre Since 1895*, Cambridge: Cambridge University Press.

Klein, N. (2007) *The Shock Doctrine: The Rise of Disaster Capitalism*, New York: Knopf.

Kolbert, E. (2007) *Field Notes from a Catastrophe: A Frontline Report on Climate Change*, London: Bloomsbury.

Kostova, L. (2000) 'Inventing Post-Wall Europe: Vision of "Old" Continent in Contemporary British Fiction and Drama', *Yearbook of European Studies*, 15: 83–102.

Kritzer, A.H. (2008) *Political Theatre in Post-Thatcher Britain, 1995–2005*, London: Palgrave.

Lesser, W. (1997) *A Director Calls: Stephen Daldry and the Theatre*, London: Faber & Faber.

Lewis, L. (2007) *Cross-Racial Casting*, Sydney: Currency Press.

Legates, M. (2001) *A History of Feminism in Western Society*, London: Routledge.

Little, R. and McLaughlin, E. (2007) *The Royal Court Theatre: Inside Out*, London: Oberon.

Luckhurst, M. (2006a) *Dramaturgy: A Revolution in Theatre*, Cambridge: Cambridge University Press.

——(ed.) (2006b) *Modern British and Irish Drama, 1880–2005*, Oxford: Blackwell.

Luckhurst, M. and Morin, E. (eds.) (2014) *Theatre and Ghosts: Materiality, Performance and Modernity*, London: Palgrave.

Laing, R.D. (1965) *The Divided Self*, Harmondsworth: Penguin.

Macey, D. (2007) *Frantz Fanon: A Life*, London: Granta.

Machon, J. (2009) *(Syn)aesthetics: Redefining Visceral Performance*, London: Palgrave.

Macintosh, K.L. (2013) *Human Cloning: Four Fallacies and their Legal Consequences*, Cambridge: Cambridge University Press.

Maitland, S. (1988) *Very Heaven: Looking Back at the Sixties*, London: Virago.

Marwick, A. (1998) *The Sixties: Cultural Revolution in Britain, France, Italy, and the United States, c.1958–c.1974*, Oxford: Oxford University Press.

Megson, C. (ed.) (2012) *Modern British Playwriting: The 1970s*, London: Methuen.

Millett, K. (1970) *Sexual Politics*, New York: Doubleday.

Milling, J. (ed.) (2012) *Modern British Playwriting: The 1980s*, London: Methuen.

Morton, A.L. (1970) *The World of the Ranters*, London: Laurence and Wishart.

Mount, F. (2012) *The New Few or A Very British Oligarchy*, London and New York: Simon and Schuster.

Nairn, T. (1977) *The Break-up of Britain: Crisis and Neo-Nationalism*, London: New Left Books.

Nicholson, S. (ed.) (2012) *Modern British Playwriting: The 1960s*, London: Methuen.

Oddey, A. (2005) *Performing Women*, London: Routledge.

Pacepa, I.M. (1988) *Red Horizons: The Extraordinary Memoirs of a Communist Spy Chief*, London: Heinemann.

Phillips, A. (1998) 'Sameness is All', in M.C. Nussbaum and C.R. Sunstein (eds.) *Clones and Clones: Facts and Fantasies about Home Cloning*, New York: Norton.

Rady, M. (1992) *Romania in Turmoil*, London and New York: I.B. Tauris.

Rayner, A. (2006) *Ghosts: Death's Double and the Phenomena of Theatre*, Minneapolis: University of Minnesota.

Rebellato, D. (1999) *1956 and All That: The Making of Modern British Drama*, London: Routledge.

Rebellato, D. (ed) (2013) *Modern British Playwriting: 2000–2009*, London: Methuen.

Rees, R. (1992) *Fringe First: Pioneers of Fringe Theatre on Record*, London: Oberon.

Reinelt, J. (1996) 'Beyond Brecht: Britain's New Feminist Drama', in H. Keyssar (ed.), *Feminist Theatre and Theory*, Basingstoke: Macmillan.

Rich, A. (1976) *Of Woman Born: Motherhood as Experience and Institution*, Washington, DC, and New York: Norton.

Richardson, K., Steffen, W. and Liverman, D. (2011) *Climate Change*, Cambridge: Cambridge University Press.

Roberts, P. (1986) *The Royal Court Theatre, 1965–1972*, Cambridge: Cambridge University Press.

——(1999) *The Royal Court Theatre and the Modern Stage*, Cambridge: Cambridge University Press.

Rohde, D. (2012) *The Betrayal and Fall of Srebrenica*, London: Penguin.

Russell, P.L. (2006) 'Trauma, Repetition and Affect', *Contemporary Psychoanalysis*, 42(4): 601–20.

Sandberg, S. (2013) *Lean In: Women, Work, and the Will to Lead*, New York: Knopf.

Seldon, A. (2007) *Blair's Britain, 1997–2007*, Cambridge: Cambridge University Press.

Shellard, D. (1999) *British Theatre Since the War*, New Haven and London: Yale University Press.

Shepard, T. (2008) *The Invention of Decolonisation: The Algerian War and the Remaking of France*, Ithaca: Cornell.

Skrimshire, S. (2010) *Future Ethics: Climate Change and the Apocalyptic Imagination*, London: Continuum.

Sontag, S. (1996) *Under the Sign of Saturn*, London: Vintage.

——(2003) *Regarding the Pain of Others*, New York: Farrar, Straus, Giroux.

Stokes, G. (1993) *The Walls Came Tumbling Down: The Collapse of Communism in Eastern Europe*, Oxford: Oxford University Press.

Stora, B. (2005) *La gangrène et l'oubli: la memoire de la guerre algérienne*, Paris: Decouverte.

Subotic, J. (2011) 'Expanding the Scope of Post-Conflict Justice: Individual, State and Societal Responsibility for Mass Atrocity', *Journal of Peace Research*, 48: 157–69.

Thomsen, C. (1981) 'Three Socialist Playwrights: John McGrath, Caryl Churchill, Trevor Griffiths', in C.W.E. Bigsby (ed.), *Contemporary English Drama*, London: Edward Arnold.

Trussler, S. (1981) *New Theatre Voices of the Seventies*, London and New York: Methuen.

Urban, K. (2004) 'Towards a Theory of Cruel Britannia: Coolness, Cruelty and the 90s', *New Theatre Quarterly* 20(4): 354–72.

Vetlesen, A.J. (2000) 'Genocide: A Case for the Responsibility of the Bystander', *Journal of Peace Research*, 37: 519–32.

Vulliamy, E. (1994) *Seasons in Hell: Understanding the Bosnian War*, London: St Martin's Press.

——(1999) 'Neutrality and the Absence of Reckoning: A Journalist's Account', *Journal of International Affairs*, 52(2): 603–20.

Willcocks, G. (2007) 'Europe in Flux: Refugees and Migration in 1990s British Plays' in N. Holdsworth and M. Luckhurst (eds.), *The Companion to Contemporary British and Irish Drama*, Oxford: Blackwell.

Williams, J. (2003) *Gilles Deleuze's* Difference and Repetition: *A Critical Introduction and Guide*, Edinburgh: Edinburgh University Press.

Wilmut, Ian, Campbell, Ian and Tudge, Colin (2000) *The Second Creation: The Age of Biological Control by the Scientists who Cloned Dolly*, London: Headline.

Index

Note: page references in *italics* refer to illustrations; n = note